About the Author

Robert Hall is an independent consultant on resilience. He was the Executive Director (2018–2021) and then Director of Strategy (2021–2022) at Resilience First Ltd, which he helped co-found. This is a not-for-profit organisation promoting business community resilience in urban areas. He also served as the Research and Policy Coordinator (2021–2022) for the National Preparedness Commission. He left both positions in May 2022.

Previously, he was Director of the Security & Resilience Network (2013–2018) at London First Ltd and before that Director of Resilience (2012–2013) at G4S Risk Management Consulting. He has also held senior positions in risk and security departments at Barclays, BAT and Marsh. He was Head of Analysis (1997–2000) at the National Criminal Intelligence Service and Managing Editor (1992–1997) of intelligence titles at Jane's Information Group, an international defence publishing company.

He founded and was Chief Executive (2000–2002) of the Global Forum on Law Enforcement and National Security (LENS) for senior executives in government, business and academia.

He has authored numerous articles in a variety of publications on strategic risk, security and resilience issues. He wrote a chapter in *Nordic Security at the Turn of the Twenty-First Century* (Zoppo, C. E. (ed.), Greenwood, 1991, ISBN: 0313275769) and a chapter in *Strategizing Resilience and Reducing Vulnerability* (Trim, P. (ed.), Nova Science, 2009, ISBN: 9781607416937).

Robert spent his early career as an officer (1974–1992) in the British Army. He served in Great Britain, Northern Ireland, Cyprus and Germany. Based on his work in the Ministry of Defence, followed by a defence fellowship, he authored *Soviet Military Art in a Time of Change: Command and Control of the Future Battlefield* (Brassey's, 1991, ISBN: 0080413218). Other books by the author are listed on pages 172-177.

He has a Bachelor of Science (Hons) degree in Zoology from the University of Bristol, a Post-Graduate Certification in Education from the University of Cardiff, and a Master of Social Science degree in Russian and East European Studies from the University of Birmingham.

Robert Hall

The Resilience Mindset

A Philosophical Journey

Austin Macauley Publishers
LONDON * CAMBRIDGE * NEW YORK * SHARJAH

Copyright © Robert Hall 2025

The right of Robert Hall to be identified as author of this work has been asserted by the author in accordance with sections 77 and 78 of the Copyright, Designs and Patents Act 1988.

All rights reserved. No part of this publication may be reproduced, stored in a retrieval system, or transmitted in any form or by any means, electronic, mechanical, photocopying, recording, or otherwise, without the prior permission of the publishers.

Any person who commits any unauthorised act in relation to this publication may be liable to criminal prosecution and civil claims for damages.

The work and words are the author's alone.

A CIP catalogue record for this title is available from the British Library.

ISBN 9781035878284 (Paperback)
ISBN 9781035878291 (ePub e-book)

www.austinmacauley.com

First Published 2025
Austin Macauley Publishers Ltd®
1 Canada Square
Canary Wharf
London
E14 5AA

Acknowledgements

I would like to thank the many people who contributed directly or indirectly to the thoughts that went into this book.

My sincere thanks go to John Deverell CBE for kindly writing the Foreword at a busy time.

Thanks also go to Steve Burns at New Trader U for his kind permission to use the image on the cover of this book. The bust depicts the Roman Emperor and philosopher Marcus Aurelius.

Any errors in the text are entirely the responsibility of the author.

My wife, Hilary, and daughter, Lisa Marie, have constantly encouraged and shared my interest in resilience.

Pre-Publication Reviews

'Skilled, competent and confident people are the foundation of effective risk and emergency management. And yet too much of what is published on resilience practice is about machinery and process, too little on people. Unlike in other fields, the body of wisdom on the inherent virtues, values and aptitudes which should be demonstrated by those in whom we place our trust to look after us in a crisis is too limited. This book is an important contribution to closing that gap, and a valuable primer and stimulus to those who want to think deeply about the competences we should expect in our resilience leaders, and how those should be reflected in their selection, training and assessment.'

Bruce Mann *is the Strategic Adviser on Risk and Resilience to the UK Covid-19 Inquiry, Commissioner on the National Preparedness Commission, and former Director of the UK's Civil Contingencies Secretariat.*

'In glorious arrogance, each generation imagines that they are experiencing issues for the first time in history: resilience is no exception. From the IRA bombings in the City of London and the "Ring of Steel" to 9/11, 7/7, Madrid, Bali, and

Istanbul, the concept of resilience has changed from random terrorist bomb atrocities to the recognition that fire, water, economic catastrophe and nature all present challenges to resilience in its many guises.

Robert blows away the myth that resilience is a modern phenomenon and examines the concept from the ancients to today. Intellectually stimulating and challenging, *The Resilience Mindset* lends stimulation to an ongoing debate on an issue that affects and impacts upon us all culturally, socially, politically and economically. Wars have been fought because of it, regimes changed. *The Resilience Mindset* represents a major contribution to what it is!'

Richard Barnes *is the former Statutory Deputy Major of London, former Board Member of Resilience First, and Board Member of UK's Cross-sector Safety and Security Communications.*

Table of Contents

Foreword	**13**
Chapter 1 Introduction	**18**
Chapter 2 Being Stoical	**33**
Chapter 3 Facing Our Fears	**48**
Chapter 4 Realising Our Virtues	**67**
Chapter 5 Finding Our Values	**87**
Chapter 6 Seeking Trust and Truth	**105**
Chapter 7 Coping with Change	**118**
Chapter 8 From Mindset to Skillset	**133**
Chapter 9 Sojourn	**155**
Other Books	**172**
Building Resilient Futures (2023)	*172*
The Triptych (2024)	*174*
Nature's Resilience (2025)	*176*
References	**178**
Index	**201**

Life can only be understood backwards but it must be lived forwards.

– Søren Kierkegaard, Danish philosopher (d. 1855)

Foreword

**by
John Deverell CBE**

This book is a valuable addition to the published body of work that deals with resilience in the face of a multitude of modern crises, whether COVID-19, climate change, supply-side challenges brought about by regional wars, or many other dramas as yet unnamed but sure to come. Much of the thinking within provides new perspectives on these challenges, and it is those perspectives that make this book such a thoroughly worthwhile read.

Furthermore, the author's practical bent—a product of decades spent on the 'front line' in one form or another—means that he has successfully created a useful guide to the subject. Following his tips, both you and your organisation can become more resilient in the face of today's pressures. As the author reminds us, it tends to be not the crises themselves but the way in which you handle them that determines whether you sink or swim.

By reminding the reader that accurate definitions are important if we are to prepare ourselves properly, the book carefully defines what is meant by resilience. It becomes clear that we often use the word far too loosely. With an appropriate and respectful nod to Nassim Taleb, author of *The Black Swan* (2007) and *Antifragile* (2012), this author makes it clear that simply being robust or resistant is not enough. That is if we want to thrive as well as survive, meaning that we need to move forward and not just return to where we were before the crisis. This is not least because the situation will likely have changed, and we need to change with it.

Clearly, the mindset that we need to develop is all important. In doing so, the author summarises the relevant elements of religious thinking and philosophy as it has developed over the ages including Stoicism that, as he explains, means so much more than simply tolerating adversity. Thus, he points the way to the utility of mindfulness, another term that means very different things to different people. Again, we are reminded that we need to be specific if we are to take the matter of resilience as seriously as we must.

The exploration of the attributes of perception, adaptability and agility develops into a valuable discussion of the differences between values and virtues—Taleb reminds us that 'Courage is the only virtue you cannot fake'—with which we need to equip ourselves to be resilient. It is the 'hard skills' referred to in the book that constitute the policies and procedures that organisations need to have in order to navigate crises. Yet, as those of us who deal with crises for our living know well, it is not feasible for organisations to have a detailed plan for every conceivable eventuality. Hence, without the complementary 'soft skills'—albeit harder to acquire—such as good leadership, adherence to principles and a 'hopeful vision', organisations may survive but will struggle to thrive.

Those soft skills, along with the appropriate mindset, need to rest on a solid foundation of truth and trust. We are reminded that both truth and trust are essential if people are to feel confident that they are bound together in a common cause. Leaders can only be effective if they understand the importance of trust—and then work hard to nurture it—which, as we know all too well, is sadly often not the case.

Trust depends on a certain tolerance of risk by leaders including the risk that those employees whom they have empowered to take decisions on behalf of their organisations might make mistakes. Those mistakes, unless particularly egregious or too often repeated, should be a basis for learning rather than punishment. In effect, to move forward entails a degree of risk-taking but risks should be taken with due consideration rather than recklessness. At the other end of the scale, a zero-risk culture is stifling and inhibits both trust and progress.

With his upcoming book (*Nature's Resilience* (2025)) in mind, the author considers Charles Darwin's theory of natural selection. While that theory embraces many different aspects such as redundancy—an important lesson that we might learn from the animal kingdom which might be summarised as 'just in case' rather than 'just in time'—it is too facile to summarise the theory as the survival of the fittest or, as some hardline employers might advocate, a dog-eat-dog mentality. Rather, the essence of Darwin is much more about developing an ability to adapt quickly to new circumstances. It is this ability that we need to develop, both individually and collectively, if we are to be truly resilient rather than concentrating on the notion of survival of the fittest. The latter is too simplistic an ethos to be a basis for dealing with today's rapidly changing world.

In terms of adaptability, the young have a head start on the rest of us. Criticisms of the younger generation as 'snowflakes' miss the point that they are more likely than the older generation to be agile and open to change. Diversity, another concept that can be prey to lazy definitions and that often gets bad press, is also valuable as a component of an organisation because it enables different points of view in the face of groupthink and wishful thinking—tendencies that have led to many a failure when navigating crises. Accordingly, the author rightly promotes an ethos of stakeholder value rather than concentrating on what constitutes shareholder value. In essence, we need to look at our environment through a broader prism, taking into account a more diverse set of criteria that reflects what really matters to people and the planet including in the longer term.

As we all know, one of the aspects of being human that constrains our willingness to change is fear. At least, that is the word the author uses, though whether anxiety might be a more appropriate word is a moot point. In any event, my memory of the motto of the British military's parachute training school is apposite: 'Knowledge dispels fear'. Hence, we need to gain an understanding of where we need to go— to anticipate—rather than travel blindly or just follow the crowd. We need to have 'the prepared mind' as Louis Pasteur described it.

That said, simply having foresight and accepting the need to change are not enough by themselves. Change or transformation without being able to sustain it will not ensure success. The author quotes Machiavelli's *The Prince* (1532):

'There is nothing more difficult to take in hand, more perilous to conduct, or more uncertain in its success, than to take the lead in the introduction of a new order of things. Because the innovator has for enemies all those who have done well under the old conditions and lukewarm defenders in those who may do well under the new.'

That reminds us that transformation is not easy and requires us to be persistent while at the same time being open to suggestions and prepared to adapt our plans accordingly. All of which demands good communication and listening skills, self-awareness, an acceptance of accountability when things go wrong, as well as a good dose of humility. These are the sort of qualities that make good leaders and are sadly all too often absent.

The overall tone of this book is one of a hopeful vision, of optimism but optimism that is based on solid foundations. In that regard, the book is not only interesting and enjoyable but also most useful as a practical guide to anyone who aspires to help build successful and happy teams and to lead well, of which the right sort of resilience is a key component.

John Deverell CBE is the Founder of The Prepared Mind. (The Prepared Mind is a division of CulturesConnect Ltd. www.thepreparedmind.net) He is a former brigadier in the British Army and currently advises the UK government on activities in conflict areas. He also advises companies on risk, business continuity, leadership and governance.

Chapter 1
Introduction

The business of philosophy is not to give rules but to analyse the private judgements of common reason.
– Immanuel Kant

COVID-19 shone a spotlight on our world. A particle visible only with an electron microscope, namely a virus with the cryptic designation SARS-CoV-2, had a catastrophic impact on the world's population—between six and twenty million died and many more millions were directly affected. The pandemic happened without any significant destruction of property or even a shot being fired across borders, the traditional culprit of mass killings.

In a perverse way, the disease outbreak was an example of the Lorenz concept, named after Edward Lorenz, a meteorology professor at the Massachusetts Institute of Technology. His founding principle of chaos theory came to be popularly known as the 'butterfly effect' after he suggested that the flap of a butterfly's wings might ultimately cause a tornado in another part of the world.[1] The flutter of a pathogen in Wuhan (China) resulted in a prolific and protracted viral storm around the globe.

The world's economy was thrown into turmoil by COVID-19, our working patterns were changed irrevocably, and sickness continues to blight the recovery of long-COVID sufferers. While a pandemic had long been predicted by scientists—if not the precise cause, symptoms or timing—and some trends in hybrid working were already taking shape, the catastrophic consequences have provided salutary lessons of the way nature can suddenly rear up and bite us badly.

With other zoonotic diseases appearing as people interface more closely with a depleted natural world, there is every reason to believe that another pandemic will appear before too long—it is not a case of if but when. In the meantime, other systemic risks will test us. Climate change must top that list and may well test us to destruction. The duration of the Anthropocene epoch is yet to be recorded.

Paradoxically, COVID-19 has shown that we can be both fragile and flexible at the same time to severe dangers. Despite advances in health care around the world over the years, we have all been susceptible to the virus. That is until vaccines appeared specific to the pathogen. We succumbed but not equally so as those vaccines were unevenly distributed around the globe and ethnic background played a part. Hopefully, immunity levels in many will have been enhanced because of inoculation programmes. These medical interventions against one danger may make us less fragile to infection from another danger in the future, an effect the author Nassim Taleb calls 'antifragile'.[2]

Taleb uses the term when something actually becomes stronger when it is damaged: think, for example, of bones or muscles which grow stronger due to external load or repeated exercise, the so-called Wolff's Law.[3] Yet, our immunity to

COVID-19 will not last forever and a new virus may appear that requires a reformulated vaccine.

We have also been relatively quick to bounce back—as well as forward—in the post-pandemic period. In many countries, economies have returned to near pre-COVID levels and employment has dipped only marginally. The world rolls on, striving for ever more growth and productivity. This is despite witnessing the first European war in nearly eighty years and all the damaging disruptions to the supplies of energy, foodstuffs and fertilisers that flow from that ongoing conflict.

A conflict in the Middle East and tensions over Taiwan only add to the global perturbations. Again, climate change could waylay any return to 'normality', exacerbated by growing and widespread mass migration as arable land becomes either flooded or shrivelled. Mitigation and resilience will be called upon to lessen the impacts.

There is little doubt that our redeeming measures will face escalating complexity and challenge. With eight billion people on the planet, a growing and intricate web of connections and relationships, ambiguous political tensions and power dynamics, as well as a volatile geosphere, there is an inevitable litany of shock and stresses (both known and unknown) to derail us in part or whole. Chronic threats like climate change, disruptive artificial intelligence, unrestricted migration, and resource depletion will be hard to resolve holistically while there is a rejection of global governance and widespread political disunity.

We can overcome these negatives—undoubtedly, a tall order—by being imaginative and proactive. As the UN Secretary-General's Report *Our Common Agenda* (2021) states: 'Our success in finding solutions to the interlinked problems we face hinges on our ability to anticipate, prevent and prepare for major risks to come.'[4]

Yet time and tide are against the methodical approach. For the first time in a century, parents cannot be assured that their children will have a better life than themselves. Beyond the specific risks and challenges, there is a general malaise and frustration over the collective failings of governments to tackle the key issues of our time. There is what has been termed a 'recession of the spirit' as the majority of people struggle with daily life and see no easy remedies.

An increasing number of people are despairing—it is the age of anxiety. The number of young people in the UK admitted to hospital for self-harming has risen by almost 70 per cent in a decade, while the number of young patients with eating disorders has doubled in three years. Suicide rates have also increased: around three-quarters were males, with those aged fifty to fifty-four having the highest rate.

Uncertainty in a turbulent world and a natural fear of change lead many to look for ready answers in populist figures who spin easy but contorted messages. Alternative lifestyles and conspiratorial theories abound, spread by social media and largely unchallenged by weak leadership models. Populism is gaining ground, especially from the right, and fragmentation of parties and communities is strengthening anti-establishment voices. Those communities are also suffering from workplace pressures and family tensions. Traditional bonds have been weakened because of cost-of-living crises and instability in familial relationships.

Resilience is one process or capacity that can help cope with this volatile and uncertain world. It is not designed to provide solutions to the causes of the shocks and stresses, but rather to establish a baseline from which to operate, recover and move forward. In simple terms, it is about surviving <u>and</u> thriving. Coming with this simplicity is the notion of preparing for and recovering from disruption so as to be able not only to anticipate but also to adapt to the change that any disruption brings.

Here is the recognition that the *status quo ante* is no longer relevant (because of change) and modifications are necessary to deal with the new set of circumstances and to better prepare for the next change. In this regard, resilience inspires growth as the experience of challenge often instils the emergence of a better person or situation—the so-called building back better strategy.[5]

The word 'resilience' was introduced into the English language in the early seventeenth century from the Latin verb *resilire* meaning to rebound or recoil. The basis of *resilire* is *salire*, a verb meaning 'to leap' which implies a bounce forward not just back. In fact, the interpretation of resilience has shifted over time from a static approach about controlling shocks by resisting them and returning to equilibrium, to a dynamic approach about overcoming shocks by moving towards a new stable equilibrium that may even be transformational; hence, the leap. This shift in emphasis has been accompanied by a growing interest in scientific publications in all fields on the topic of resilience but especially in social sciences and policymaking.[6]

It is important at the start of this journey to distinguish resilience from two other related elements, namely robustness and resistance. Robustness refers to strength and effectiveness in adverse conditions; it is the capacity to endure. The important point is that robustness means there is minimal impact or change despite the external pressures whereas resilience implies there is change and a new status.

A complex network can be robust if it keeps its basic functionality even when some of its components fail. A bridge is robust, for example, if it can withstand the regular traffic flow under all weathers without deforming. Similarly, a person is robust if he or she can continue with a project even if the working conditions are harsh and unfavourable.

Robustness generally occurs prior to resilience—protection first, then recovery. Interestingly, interpreters of the speeches of President Putin translate resilience with the Russian word *ustoichivost* which means robustness. This is probably because Russian official discourse is centred around the idea of stability, portraying it as the absence of shocks and crises, while resilience particularly describes the reaction to shocks.[7]

While robustness refers to the inherent capacity for toughness and durability unaffected by a disturbance (a largely passive response), resistance reflects a fight back to maintain the *status quo* or equilibrium (a more active response). Both prevent the disturbance from shutting down processes or activities and amount to a defensive and protective posture—the resolute digging in rather than the brazen assault.

Resistance to external forces can be witnessed when an individual or population comes under attack or there is a danger of potential harm. It refers to the ability of an individual or community to withstand a shock or stress and assumes that there is no major reorganisation or successional change involved. It is an obvious first response to resist and protect. It may even stimulate an immune reaction to defeat an invading foreign body when and where such immunity exists. While resistance can generally be positive, it can have a downside if it becomes an end in itself, and dogged becomes dogmatic: it should not turn into stubbornness or inaction by denying the process of change when the situation demands or allows. Such resistance can deny resilience.

By way of contrast, resilience implies that there is some level of readjustment or reorganisation in the face of disruption while retaining essentially the same function, structure, identity and feedback, perhaps through a mosaic of patches that are at different stages of reassembly. This corresponds with the Chinese view of resilience which is conceptualised as both the adaptability of the weak against the resilience of the strong, as well as the development of perseverance through adversity.

As we will explore, and the title of this book alludes to, resilience—whether professional or personal—requires an appropriate mindset if it is to be effective. A mindset is a set of beliefs that shapes how individuals make sense of the world and themselves. It is formed by values, attitudes, culture, responsibilities and experiences which, in turn, shape the way we incorporate new knowledge and how we respond to a wide range of situations.

As people encounter different situations, the brain triggers a specific mindset that directly impacts behaviour towards that situation. A mindset influences how one thinks, feels and responds in any given situation. It means that what you believe about yourself impacts your success or failure. According to American psychologist Carol Dweck in her book *Mindset* (2007), your beliefs play a pivotal role in what you want and whether you achieve it.[8]

The use of the word mindset introduces the broader notion of philosophy, the subtitle of this book. In stark terms, philosophy is a theory of attitudes that acts as a guiding principle for behaviour. It is a thought process that people undertake to understand the fundamental truths about themselves, the world in which they live, and their relationship with one another. It offers an insight into how we can live better lives. Through it, we can train our minds to see patterns by joining disparate dots and thereby make connections.

Philosophy asks those essential questions about existence (metaphysics), reason (logic), knowledge (epistemology), value (axiology), mind and language. As we live in a world of constant change, both self-imposed and inflicted, philosophy can help us understand how to cope positively and rise to the inevitable challenges. It is why philosophy down the ages has attracted students who want a deeper appreciation of resilience. Ultimately, it is the resilience of the human spirit that gives hope to human endeavours.

If we are to understand the mindset that surrounds resilience, it is necessary to go back to founding principles and underlying motives. Philosophy, especially that forged in the Hellenistic period (323–30 BC), has a great deal to say that is relevant to today's challenges, and we ignore the wisdom expressed by ancestors at our peril. This journey begins therefore with a look at the writings of some of the ancient Greeks and Roman thinkers, people who are often referred to as the Stoics. (*Chapter 2*) They have much to say about the ideas behind resilience or, as they would prefer to call it, Stoicism. Today, we use the adjectives stoic and stoical to refer to a person who displays resilience.

The Greeks did not believe that moving forward into the future was like crossing a field. They thought that you cannot step forward into the future since you cannot know what the next moment will be until after it has occurred. There was no precognition. 'The only way to move into the future is by looking backwards, as if sitting in the back of a moving boat, looking out over the wake, seeing the next moment only after we have passed through it.'[9] 'Walking backward toward the future, with our eyes facing in the opposite direction from which we are moving, we can stare far into what has already passed, lining up recent past events with distant past events for the greater clarification of both; we just can't turn around.'

While such philosophy provides a starting point, it has subsequently been nuanced and adapted, even rejected. People want to look ahead but to learn from the past. As the opening quotation by the renowned Danish philosopher Søren Kierkegaard suggests, we must look at the past in order to cope with the present and the future. The Uruguayan writer Pablo Vierci, who was behind the acclaimed survival film *Society of the Snow* (2023), believes that: 'We have to return to the past, knowing that the past is what changes us the most.'[10]

Our natural curiosity to peer into the fog of the horizon, no matter how hard to penetrate, provides a basis for enquiry and innovation. At the same time, we need to be aware that past trends will not necessarily be replicated going forward, particularly in any period of transformation. This is why philosophical thinking is not limited to classical writings or determined by renowned contributors. It can and does apply to our current approach to resilience and attendant attributes like agility, adaptation, leadership and perception.

Resilience by itself, however, will not provide the alternatives and answers. This is because resilience per se is a process or journey for preparing for and dealing with or adapting to perturbations. In other words, the expectation of disruption is there and cannot be wished away. It is a case of how we approach the interruptions.

We need to develop a mindset and culture—both behavioural and organisational—that promote resilience and create a spear as well as a shield, defences that allow people to cope with and overcome the resulting challenges whatever they might be. This is where Stoicism has much to offer as a starting point, but it is also pertinent for the modern era: it is a way to build resilience.

Any examination of resilience would be incomplete without considering the philosophy of fear in the context of risk tolerance. (*Chapter 3*) Why have we become so risk-averse, almost to the point where we can be paralysed or restricted from acting? This is despite having ever more tools and information at hand to stave off disaster. Early warning systems abound while artificial intelligence and quantum technologies can help with advanced notification short of prediction. The dilemma of knowing the facts but fearing the consequences was well expressed by Aaron Wildavsky, an American political scientist, who remarked that: 'The richest, longest lived, best protected, most resourceful civilisation with the highest degree of insight into its own technology, is on its way to becoming the most frightened. Has there ever been, one wonders, a society that produced more uncertainty more often about everyday life?'[11]

Part of the problem may lie in overestimating the dangers. Even the Stoics had something to say about 'groundless fears'.[12] The situation has certainly become more intense since the time Wildavsky wrote his analysis in the late 1970s. We need therefore to ask why and what can be done. Transitioning from an over-emphasis on analysis and interpretation of the risks (the causes) themselves to a greater appreciation and management of the impacts (the consequences) of those risks could bring us closer to finding practical, resilient solutions.

As capabilities and resources will rarely be sufficient to cope with the multiple challenges, particularly if they become concurrent or colliding, the solutions may well require a mindset that moves away from a constant obsession with growth and power to one that focuses on outcomes and values, using the assets available. It would require a philosophical shift to what can be described as the 'benediction of enough'.[13]

Effective responses can also require better situational awareness and increased knowledge sharing as these two characteristics can help remove doubt and uncertainty, and hence fear. It was the American novelist Herman Melville who wrote in *Moby Dick* (1851): 'Ignorance is the parent of fear.' But information and knowledge are not automatic features even for an advanced civilisation in the modern age. Fear and superstition remain powerful forces and combine to ensure that humanity is not inevitably enlightened; it can regress in art, architecture, literature, and even science.[14]

To realise potential and progress, there are fundamental elements that first need to be in place. The journey begins with a discussion of virtues. (*Chapter 4*) This may sound an old-fashioned approach but virtues are universal, timeless attributes that set out right from wrong: they offer a moral compass. Some would argue that the weakening of the magnet is allowing our modern compass to falter in showing the right direction. We are in danger of losing our morality and humanity in the face of competing demands that position wealth and status ahead of equality and empathy.

Here, the ancient Platonic and Aristotelian cardinal virtues of wisdom, courage, moderation and justice come to our rescue. They can shape resilience and each has something to contribute in shaping the resilience mindset.

Virtues also influence values which most people hold dear and which are commonly described by organisations as their *raison d'être* for service or production. Values are those goals, ideals or even opinions that are considered important in setting the tone and culture of everyday transactions and behaviour. (*Chapter 5*) They are principles, often subjective and personal, that can help one to decide what is important in life. Values should therefore be lived and acted upon, unlike virtues which should be experienced and observed. Values may be stated or unstated but it is reasonable to ask how many are put into practice and followed. A resilience mindset requires a clear set of values to follow in challenging times.

When discussing values and virtues, philosophers regularly raise the issues of trust and truth. (*Chapter 6*) These are not necessarily directly related but essential psychological elements if resilience is to be effective and has a chance of maturing. The Stoics appreciated truthfulness and honesty as virtues. Current and growing political and societal polarisation, exacerbated by social media, allows misrepresentation and misinformation to become easy infiltrators. Amid the tumult, however, there may be signs of hope.

A report by Ipsos concluded that despite a year (2022) of negative news, political uncertainty and economic woe, 'the bedrock of trust that the world's population has in government and the major industry sectors of the world is still improving slowly, in most cases.'[15] A later survey, the *2024 Edelman Trust Barometer*, shows overall trust around the world to make sure innovations are safe, understood and accessible is largely stable, even with economic headwinds.[16] Trust with the business sector is greater than with NGOs, government or the media, but overall there has been a decline of authority from the previous year.

The fact that there is an unprecedented period of change underway in many walks of life—making resistance understandable, particularly as societal attitudes harden—coping with change, whether psychological or physical, is an appropriate topic to study next. (*Chapter 7*) Agility and adaptation are two characteristics that cannot only help deal with change but also allow new opportunities and ways of working to be realised. They are the embodiments of resilience. Agility requires a mental ability to think laterally and often quickly, to be innovative as well as curious. To achieve this, there needs to be fluid boundaries so that people can use their initiative and explore new horizons out of the box.

Adaptability can be viewed as the application of agility as it is the implementation of that new thinking in novel ways of being and behaving. Many philosophies, both Western and Eastern, have emphasised the idea that because the world is in a constant state of flux then individuals need to cultivate a flexible mindset and adapt to the changing circumstances.

Developing the resilience mindset into a skillset is the ultimate deliverable. (*Chapter 8*) The question is how we can best prepare people philosophically and practically to be ready for a portfolio of jobs in their working lives. Persistent change in the world of work will make constant reskilling or upskilling important and necessary. While there will be certain crucial meta-skills such as communication and knowledge that will be constant throughout life's journey, there will be some skills that will help particularly with developing a resilience mindset. Philosophers down the ages have placed, for instance, a strong emphasis on social or people skills to navigate life, those essential soft skills such as compassion, kindness, integrity and fairness.

Fostering trusted relationships, for example, should also be a strong feature of resilience but it requires consistency, transparency, respect, equality and responsibility (alongside rights). These skills are at least equal to, perhaps arguably more so, the hard skills of policies and procedures. Both hard and soft skills can be acquired beyond raw experience.

Resilience is a journey as there is no destination or final goal. In the final part of this book, a series of milestones are offered that summarise the journey the reader has taken throughout these pages. (*Chapter 9*) They are route markers that identify the important scenes along the resilience road. An overriding message is that we can never become fully resilient as change is constantly happening to present new dilemmas and challenges. With a deepening sense of political polarisation, societal atomisation and economic inequity, it is impossible to have a single file ready for every eventuality.

It will often be the least expected crisis that occurs next and that may well be concurrent with other crises. This idea has given rise to the notion of permacrisis or poly-crisis, contributing to an age of emergencies. To be able to cope and be stoical, we need a set of guidelines to steer us through the morass. This will be neither quick nor easy, but hopefully, this book casts some light on the road ahead. If Edward O Wilson, an American socio-biologist, was right when he said that 'We have Palaeolithic emotions, mediaeval institutions and God-like technology,' we need all the light we can generate and have a long way still to travel.[17]

The book is the second in a series of books on resilience. The first book, *Building Resilient Futures* (2023), looked at what resilience means at times of crisis as well as the in-between periods. It examined the various types of resilience, such as emotional, organisational, social and national, and offered insights on how to manage the consequences of upheaval and trauma.

The third book, *Nature's Resilience* (2025), considers how resilience manifests itself in the natural world and how biological resilience may help us understand our own human resilience. It features ten profiles of specific animals and plants that have developed their resilient capacities in different ways for different habitats. We may not be able to learn directly from, for example, the pine tree, the bear or the octopus, but they can reveal activities, behaviours, even chemicals or genes, that can benefit our world.

I hope you enjoy the journey.

Robert Hall
April 2024

Chapter 2
Being Stoical

You have power over your mind—not outside events. Realise this, and you will find strength.
– Marcus Aurelius

'To be stoic', a trait, is a phrase which is often used as a descriptor of resilience, a process. Stoicism implies perseverance, steadfastness, grit, determination, tenacity, mettle, spirit, and more besides. Such characteristics reflect our soul, our spirit and our human nature. In effect, Stoicism can be considered the precursor to the philosophy of resilience. If one needs a definition, the Cambridge Dictionary describes Stoicism as 'the quality of experiencing pain or trouble without complaining or showing your emotions'. This is a tall order and demanding sacrifice but with an admirable purpose.

The philosophy of Stoicism could be described as the most influential ethical doctrine of the ancient world before Christianity. Its roots lie in the ideas espoused by philosophers such as Socrates (d.399 BC), Plato (d.348 BC) and Aristotle (d.322 BC). Followers have stood on the shoulders of these philosophical giants. One was the founder of Stoicism, reportedly a Greek by the name of Zeno of

Citium (d.c264 BC) in Cyprus. He is supposed to have lectured from a porch (*stoa*), hence the origin of the movement.

The early Stoicswere disillusioned by the collapse of the Greek city-states due to a combination of inter-state conflict and the decline of the Alexandrian empire. The Stoics felt there was little hope for social reconstruction and regeneration following the absorption of the city-states into the Roman empire in 146 BC. Although many empires have come and gone, the sentiments have resonance with the current geopolitical arena. There is today a weakening of confidence in democracies around the world while the likes of China, Russia and Iran pose transnational challenges to the modern Western capitalist empire on an unprecedented and coordinated scale. Hostile invasions of neighbouring territories—personified by Russia's absorption of parts of Ukraine—are included in the recasting of a new international order.

The Stoic school taught that virtue (*virtus*) was the highest good and was based on the search for knowledge. Virtue can be characterised as a trait of excellence; it may be moral, social or intellectual. The cultivation and refinement of virtue was held to be for the 'good of humanity' and thus was valued as the purpose of life or a foundational principle of being. According to the Greeks, the wise should live virtuous lives and be indifferent to the vicissitudes of fortune or the tribulations of pleasure and pain.

The turmoil in ancient Greece encouraged the Stoics to look at the mindset of people and an individual's insight on overcoming challenges rather than seeking remedies in external domains.

As a result, the philosophy was based on reason-based virtue, individual responsibility, humility, self-control and fortitude in times of stress and uncertainty. In the words of the Stoic Epictetus (d.c135), an enslaved Roman: 'It's not what happens to you but how you react to it that matters.' It was by accepting fate (predestination) that it was possible to be independent of the vagaries of the world and to internalise the challenges. The key was to focus on what could be controlled and park the elements that could not.

Stoicism is therefore a construct based on inner strength, whether that be spiritual or secular, arising out of a sense of struggle to overcome adversity. It is the cornerstone of resilience. It is also perhaps why it is commonly associated with people suffering prolonged captivity or being subject to some form of extended duress. Accounts by such victims often mention the benefits of Stoic philosophy in helping their resilience and resistance despite hardship.

Stoicism teaches that we have power over our own minds and not outside events; it promotes resolve from within. A Stoic of virtue should amend one's will to suit the world as one finds it and not be moulded by it. This approach is based on the view that the individual should be independent of the threats around them. We may be victims of external events but we should not be dominated by them. Rather, we can through perseverance and calmness shine a light on the situation for ourselves and others around us. Here is a strong component of being able to lead others through the morass.

Even when we feel helpless in the face of horrors at home or abroad, our outlook can influence what goes on whether in a small way individually or a large way collectively. We can all play a part and thereby sustain our resilience. As the theologian and philosopher John O'Donohue wrote in *Benedictus* (2007), just before his premature demise (d.2008), '...the way you look at things is not simply a private matter. Your outlook actually and concretely affects what goes on. When you give in to helplessness, you conclude with despair and add to it. When you take back your power and choose to see the possibilities for healing and transformation, your creativity awakens and flows to become an active force of renewal and encouragement in the world.'[18] This sentiment is a powerful motivator for individuals to adopt the spirit or essence of resilience, whatever the source of that spirit may be.

The ideas of the Stoics are echoed in the philosophy of mindfulness which has Buddhist traditions. Some proponents have claimed mindfulness has enhanced both their resilience and well-being by reducing negative and harmful emotions and hence stress. The concept is essentially the ability to focus on the present moment, aware of where one is and what one is doing but not overly reacting to, or being overwhelmed by, what is going on in the background. In this regard, it is aligned with Stoical thinking as it concentrates on the instant by finding purpose and meaning which one can shape rather than the future which is less readily influenced.

Both mindfulness and resilience are valued in education and society more for their psychological benefits than their moral value. The whole concept of mindfulness has become a mainstream movement with international endorsements—some would say a panacea, even a 'conspiracy'.[19]

Whatever the inspiration, a philosophical approach that focuses on the individual rather than the circumstance is one which has given considerable shape to Western culture over the centuries. The fact that the ancient Greeks placed great value upon individual freedoms and rational thinking has matured enough to be the fount of much Western thinking and development. Their philosophy set the scene for us in the West to become more innovative, competitive and technologically advanced than other (non-Western) cultures. We may have consequentially developed a reductionist approach to problem-solving that breaks down events and activities to their fundamental elements and pigeonholes them into silos, compartments or sector-specific actions. This is done in the belief that the result gives understanding and meaning to many of our subsequent responses.

These reductionist characteristics may have helped to build personal resilience but have also caused us to concentrate and analyse (over) intently on causes and categories. However, in trying to understand complex, interrelated issues, making compartments or silos can be unhelpful as they potentially present barriers to understanding and the identification of relationships. Tom Oliver in his insightful book *The Self Delusion* (2020) notes that: 'Psychologists have found that, on balance, people from Western cultures are more likely to see events and objects in isolation, including themselves, which leads to "individualistic" attitudes.'[20]

We are self-focused and independent, prone to overestimating how much we understand and can influence the world. This may allow a degree of creativity, if not irrationality, to creep into mindsets which can be positive and improve resilience. People can often act irrationally: it is part of being human and can be a useful adaptation to uncertainty providing humility dominates arrogance.

Oliver continues: 'In contrast, people from East Asian cultures are more likely to perceive things and events as an inextricable part of a broader context and…tend to adopt "collectivist" attitudes.' Oliver accepts this is very broad stereotyping, but it holds certain truths. We tend to concentrate on flaws and disparities rather than the greater, worthier attributes. It is like looking at a masterpiece of art and focusing on the brush strokes rather than the overall message that the artist is trying to convey. To be resilient, we need to focus out as well as in: the goal is more important than the grate.

Individualism, and a creeping rejection of social responsibilities over personal rights and freedoms, is certainly testing the norms and boundaries of traditional societies. Stresses and strains are exacerbated by a widening wealth gap, weakening familial ties, growing mental ill-health, a feeling of disillusion with and dispossession from governance systems, and a growing influence of social media that not only encourages (contrary to the name) fewer face-to-face contacts but also allows personal barbs and insults. There is a danger in all this turbulence that we see personal freedom and individual rights as the rationale for disengaging with others.

Yet the Stoic philosophy is not about isolation or individual grit and endurance. Nancy Sherman in her book *Stoic Wisdom* (2021) makes the point that: 'The Stoics never believed, as some argue, that rugged self-reliance or indifference to the world around us is at the heart of living well. We are at home in the world, they insisted, when we are connected to each other in cooperative efforts. We build resilience and goodness through our deepest relationships.'[21]

Reliance on others depends on building communities of cooperation, respect and support. In fact, the Stoics were the first cosmopolitans (*kosmopolites*) or citizens of the world and thought beyond the confines of the small city-state (*polis*). They widened the common good from the *polis* to the *cosmos* in acknowledgement of being part of a greater whole.

The adoption of social interdependence built from the ground up was a strong message from another famous Stoic, the Roman Emperor and philosopher Marcus Aurelius (d.180). (See image on the front cover.) He pointed out that the human body was made up of separate limbs and organs but only functioned successfully when it operated as an integral whole.

In his collection of private diaries, *Meditations* (161–180), he portrays a severed hand or foot lying apart from the rest of the human body and asks if that is what 'man makes of himself...when he cuts himself off from the universal of which he is part'. Similarly, we cannot thrive by severing ourselves from the political and social whole of which we are part.

If we are too indifferent and independent, we are in danger of losing perspective, becoming unwell, unbalanced and indulgent. Equally importantly, we may fail to address the systemic, even existential, problems that face the human race such as climate change, technologies like artificial intelligence, or anti-microbial resistance. Again, a holistic, interdependent approach may be a better way to rise to these challenges writ large. Oliver suggests that it is time to look beyond the reductionism of Western philosophy initiated by the Stoics and look wider to holism in other cultures by acknowledging 'the seamless nature of the interconnected world'.[22]

Other modern thinkers have taken up the challenge of trying to find the balance between the independent and collective models. Martin Seligman, an American psychologist and philosopher, for example, reconciles the individualistic approach which emphasises self-care and inner strength, and the altruistic approach which emphasises sacrifice for the greater good and downplays individuality.[23] Seligman's theory of human happiness focuses on well-being and resilience, and developing a positive outlook in the face of life's challenges. His research has looked at the identification of virtues that would be helpful in mental well-being.

With holistic and altruistic approaches struggling to surface in modern times, it is appropriate that the ideas of community resilience and a whole-of-society or whole-of-nation approach should come to the fore. Such ideas involve all parts of a society in resilience, whether that be the public, private, voluntary, charity, religious, union or education sectors. The totality of engagement in the face of a major or national danger can be a force multiplier. These ideas are again not new. Marcus Aurelius routinely talked about an image of reason binding us together in 'mutually intertwined movements' that can work together, whether consciously or not: 'Things which are still superior, even though they are separated from one another, unity in a manner exists, as in the stars.'[24]

Sherman comments: 'The idea of mutual endeavour and coordination runs wide and deep' for people like Aurelius and should for other potential leaders.[25]

As a military man, Aurelius would understand the term 'doctrine' to describe the fundamental principles by which military forces intertwine their movements in order to guide their actions in support of objectives. Doctrine is authoritative but requires clear judgement in application. It has been described as: 'a common vehicle for expression and a common plane of thought.' [26] The British military has developed its joint doctrine specifically to enable all three-armed services (navy, army and air force) to operate in harmony for maximum impact, thereby becoming a force multiplier.

Beyond the military environment, the Stoic philosophy resonates with modern challenges and today's application of resilience. As in ancient times, we face a fractious, some would say crumbling, world order with globalisation on the way down and protectionism on the way up. Yet, even so, we cannot ignore the interconnectedness and interdependence of much of the world's activities: just think of the multitude of people involved in bringing your daily meal and the links in the supply chain from field to fork. Then there is climate change which no one country can solve alone. Hence, even if reshoring or onshoring gains momentum as globalisation weakens, we will remain indebted to others around the world for our sustenance and survival.

Feeling connected and not alone is something the Stoics acknowledged. They used the term *oikeiosis* which can be loosely translated as familiarisation or affiliation. Its general sense is that of belonging or being at home with oneself in the world. It has spiritual, psychological and physiological components, affecting the health and well-being of people and their environments. Tom Oliver speaks of the 'confluence of connectedness'.

It applies at all levels of human engagement. He describes, for example, how the state of our internal microbiome and genome can influence our behaviours towards external parties and even the natural world. He concludes: 'Changing our personal perspective to be aware of these extensive interconnections and develop a compassionate approach is...the first step in engendering wider change in society.'[27] In fact, those thinkers and writers who have encouraged humanity to take care of our world and the natural environment have done so largely because they themselves have been moved by a sense of wonder of the world's magnificence and concern for its preservation through cooperation. That feeling needs to be nurtured as it strengthens common bonds and cements the realisation that we are all part of the same global playing field.

Nancy Sherman points out: 'The overarching Stoic promise is that it is not the stress events, acute or chronic, that build our resilience. It is how we give those events meaning. It is our attitudes and evaluations.'[28] Again, the Stoics emphasised that strong bonds and supportive networks were all part of adaptability: it was not a solitary journey. Marcus Aurelius, for instance, recognised social interdependence—those 'mutually intertwined movements'—and tried to build support from the ground up as well as the top down. This is very much a modern aspect of leadership in resilience.

It is therefore unsurprising that now, as in ancient times, we continue to seek better alternatives (and leadership) that promise greater order and stability. The Stoics would say that the first emphasis should lie in our own approaches and mindset, and not in a mastery of outside events even if that was possible. It is judgements that affect us and not the plethora of dangers out there. This is very much at the heart of resilience which could be seen as threat agnostic.

While we should prepare ourselves, both emotionally and psychologically, for the worst, we should not be hostage to external interventions. As Nancy Sherman reminds us: 'Most current psychological studies no longer view the resilient individual as "invulnerable" but rather look at the social and cultural protective factors that promote risk and adversity adaptation.'

We should be alert to the dangers behind concepts like populism and nationalism which both have applicability today. Perhaps the concepts stem from our traditional tendency towards coalescing around tribes for security and sustenance. The most vibrant and passionate bonds come from belonging to teams, neighbourhoods, clubs and ethnic and linguistic groups, all of which tend to protect their own with vigour and determination: consider the energies of football club supporters. They are connected through a common identity and desire for success over rivals: they will remain loyal through promotions and relegations.

Belonging to a club, tribe or nation in a turbulent world is a powerful motivator and has within it a strong component of resilience. Even a prisoner of war can gain succour from having a sense of national identity. The trait can also extend to a terrorist group which might display persistence by maintaining a flexible structure around a twisted ideology despite repeated physical attacks or leadership decapitations; such resilience could be termed the 'resilience of the extremes'.[29]

Resilience breaks down, however, when power and egotism, especially narcissism, get in the way. Then superiority and supremacy cloud judgements, override the greater good and search for better collective solutions. Corrupt or conniving leaders will play on people's insecurity by providing false hope and easy solutions. Appealing to tribalistic tendencies by reinforcing inequities and exaggerating the dangers in an opponent's policies can only diminish collectivist approaches, raise inter-group tensions and weaken overall resilience. With a world of eight billion people generating a plethora of separate agendas and aspirations, it is understandably hard to reach harmony and interconnectedness.

The traditional upsides of innovation and technology in Western culture have come face to face with the modern downsides of disharmony and dysfunction in many societies. Yet, there are many serious global issues that make the search for common answers beyond tribes and nations ever more pertinent.

In terms of resilience, the Stoic philosophy opens a window on our approach to threats and risk management. The idea that we could or should be more independent of events and less blown off course by their vagaries, chimes with the notion that resilience is about an approach that should be detached from the threats around i.e., threat-neutral or agnostic.

The premise of this notion is that there are so many 'knowns' and 'unknowns' out there that it is simply impossible to have a resilient plan for each and everyone, including the unknowns. It may be wiser to adopt a general approach to our responses that will be generic and holistic, focusing on impacts and consequences across the board rather than the myriad of discrete causes. In fact, the term 'holism' is about looking for properties that are not present in the parts and not reducible to the study of parts.[30]

Jamie Shea, a former senior official (deputy assistant secretary-general) in NATO, has made the point that it would be unwise to play God by seeking to second-guess the next big shock. He said that, like a pair of swimming trunks, security can only ever cover so much at any given time so no matter how good one's horizon-scanning capabilities may they can never guarantee an entirely accurate view round the next corner. This makes it crucial to have in place 'common response elements for diverse, overlapping risks and threats'.[31]

A key question is how does a person become stoic and more resilient. There is no absolute pinnacle or final destination when perfection is achieved and retained. Rather it is a journey of incremental steps. This is why maturity models are commonly used in organisational terms to reflect progression to higher levels of resilience. There is also the question of nature versus nurture in capability.

Some people appear to have a better, innate capacity than others to cope with challenges and adversity; others learn and adapt in the face of hardship and challenge. Military training tries to improve resilience and confer that added measure of 'grit' to the character of service personnel whatever their baseline.

This is because the Stoic principles are well suited to military service and duty. Individual and collective responsibility, self-reliance, identity and fortitude are all positive traits applicable to the uniformed services. They allow self-confidence, resourcefulness, perseverance and trustworthiness to develop, both individually and in teams or units.

Once installed, they transfer to other professions and later in life. There is an age-old adage that you can take the man out of the army but you cannot take the army out of the man. The Stoic notion also makes the point that resilience is about being connected to others who invest in you and support your efforts: it is more than just individual survival and inner strength. The notion and traits have held good since Greek and Roman times, if not earlier.

Characteristics that are key to Stoicism's appeal are the idea of flexibility and adaptation. Adaptation in the face of hardship and challenge is an essential component of resilience but often ignored as it is one of the more difficult components both to articulate and implement. (Adaptation is examined further in *Chapter 7.*) It implies change—never an easy sell—and an ability to be agile in the face of changing circumstances. To be fleet of foot and mentally alert allows a rapid yet measured response to change so that it does not overwhelm in the heat of the crisis.

Beyond having confidence in oneself and trust in those around you, there is an absolute need to be empowered (at all levels) so that actions can be taken without hierarchical sanction or a fear of adverse repercussions. These are traits to be attained by training, skills and assessments before, not during, events. They will be the true measure of a positive response. Sherman concludes her assessment with these words: 'Stoicism is a way to endure and cultivate inner virtue when tight control from outside threatened your very being.'[32]

Leadership plays a crucial role in Stoic resilience. The best leaders were those who could knit together different constituencies and institutions, brokering relationships and transactions across different levels of political, economic and social organisations. (See *Chapters 5* and *8* for further discussions of leadership and governance.) They work up and down and across organisational hierarchies, connecting with groups who might otherwise be excluded, and translating between constituencies. Two writers have called such people 'translational leaders'.[33]

The presence or absence of these leaders can have a profound impact on recovery and resilience when disruption occurs as they can translate and transfer ideas across a network.

Business leaders can learn a great deal from Stoical principles and, hence, the philosophy remains very much alive and avidly studied today. It is pertinent when trying to unravel complexity as it brings one back to basics, what is important, and helps winnow the chaff from the wheat.[34] So strong is the motivation that in *Stoicism at the Summit: Embodying Ancient Principles for Peak Performance* (2023) the authors advocate building a Stoic leadership blueprint and learning culture within modern organisations as well as engaging with and strengthening the wider community along the same principles.[35]

'By grounding their ambitions in Stoic contentment and virtue, business leaders can truly achieve peak performance and leadership, driving organisations to new summits of success.' There can hardly be a better recommendation for developing a resilience mindset along such principles.

Chapter 3
Facing Our Fears

There is no fear without some hope, and no hope without some fear.
— Baruch Spinoza

According to the Stoic Epictetus, 'Philosophy's main task is to respond to the soul's cry: to make sense of and thereby free ourselves from the hold of our griefs and fears.' [36] If philosophy is to 'make sense' of our fears, as Epictetus says, so too should it give us the capacity to determine whether we have the right fears and prepare accordingly.

Tackling our fears by addressing the potential risks ahead, whether individually or collectively, is part of being resilient, that ability to bounce both back and forward in the face of life's challenges. As fear can be viewed as an emotion, a psychological response to a real or perceived danger, the response should be part of the resilience mindset. To be resilient is to front and overcome fears. Marcus Aurelius, who reverted to Epictetus for insight, wrote in *Meditations* that: 'If you are distressed by anything external, the pain is not due to the thing itself but to your estimate of it, and this you have the power to revoke at any moment.'

The earlier philosopher Epicurus (d.270 BC), who founded the Epicureanism movement of the Hellenistic age, believed that it was important to liberate people from fear not only the fear of death but also the fear of life. He believed that the one thing with the greatest power to ruin our days and lives was fear. He talked of tranquillity and the absence of fear (*ataraxia*). In his era, when all forms of public life were unpredictable and highly dangerous, Epicurus taught people to seek happiness and fulfilment.

This was completely at odds with previous ideas of seeking fame and glory. In order to achieve *ataraxia*, Epicurus stated that we needed first to understand our fears and then we could address those with which we have some control. Today, this translates into formulating risk registers and risk assessments which are traditional parts of any risk-management approach.

Too often, fears come rolling in together like a wave with no way of discerning intensity or priority. We could be thinking about the fear of our country being involved in a nuclear war at the same time as worrying about whether the supermarket has our favourite food in store. We can also escalate or misapply fears. We can hold multiple fears at the same time, with some supplanting others as circumstances change: a soldier's personal fear of battle can be replaced and overcome by fear of letting down his colleagues and unit, for instance. The philosopher Baruch Spinoza (d.1677) maintained that everyone had a basic 'fear of solitude' because each of us was helplessly alone, and hence desired order in our lives.[37]

The list of recognised individual phobias (*phobos*) is prolific.[38] Often, there is no rational explanation for those fears which does not necessarily diminish them. The facts are sometimes ignored. The danger of being killed on the road, for instance, is more than two thousand times greater than in a plane but many have a fear of flying (aerophobia).[39]

On the grander scale, some fears are explicable, and not entirely without merit. There is also the prospect of weaponising fears so that a pervasive feeling emanates across people or communities, compelling or inhibiting a course of action: illegal migration is a current topic that could fall into this category.

In his book *Fear* (2023), Robert Peckham wrote that fear was: 'both a coercive tool of power and a catalyst for radical change'.[40] There are many examples in history of both acting separately and concurrently. Nonetheless, others believe fear is an underrated factor in explaining wars over and above hatred or power. Some have argued that what propelled the European powers into war in 1914 was not greed or animosity but the gnawing fear of falling behind, of losing face and allies, of finding their countries isolated and vulnerable. It was the fear of something worse that drove the Austrians to issue their fateful ultimatum after the assassination of Archduke Ferdinand in Sarajevo, according to Christopher Clark in *The Sleepwalkers* (2013).[41]

Fear of global terrorism was the driving force after the attacks on the USA on 11 September 2001, fear of Russia's expansionism has followed the invasion of Ukraine on 24 February 2022, and fear of more attacks from Hamas after 7 October 2023 has fuelled Jewish concerns for Israel's survival. Above all these, there are existential fears of a climate meltdown and of mass migration. Other systemic fears include the deleterious effects of serious and organised crime, especially cybercrime, degenerative artificial intelligence, mass decryption with quantum computing, and yet more destabilisation from geopolitical upheavals.

Sometimes, so many fears mount up that we become paralysed or withdrawn and unable to act on any one concern. As the French diplomat and political philosopher Alexis de Tocqueville wrote in *Democracy in America* (1840): 'I cannot help fearing that men may reach a point where they look on every new theory as a danger, every innovation as a toilsome trouble, every social advance as a first step toward revolution, and that they may absolutely refuse to move at all.'[42] This view echoes that of the Stoics who believed that most fears arise from giving too much value to actions and events that we cannot control.

We may censor or try to avoid potential dangers, but this brings its own challenges. Fear can stifle innovation and cripple rational thought. It can be pervasive and pernicious, spreading throughout a team or organisation if unchecked. It can seriously undermine trust and lead to organisational and reputational fragmentation. Fear can ruin personal journeys.

The UK charity The Prince's Trust believes around half of sixteen- to twenty-five-year-olds in the UK feel daily fearful about the future while over a half thought their generation's prospects frightening and a third already felt their lives were spiralling out of control.[43] According to *The Economist*, around four-and-a-half million Britons were in contact with mental-health services in 2021–2022, a rise of almost one million in five years while the number of people who are out of work with mental-health conditions has risen by a third in 2019–2023.[44] People in their early twenties are more likely to be not working due to ill-health than those in their early forties, another report has found.[45] All this contributes to a rise in suicide rates.

The invidiousness of fear can readily generate panic and paranoia. The Canadian philosopher Brian Massumi commented in his *Politics of Everyday Fear* (1993) that: '...naturalised fear, ambient fear, ineradicable atmospheric fright has become "the discomfiting affective [music]" and we should pay "special attention" to fear to the extreme, to the great symphonies of collective hysteria, panic, and national paranoia.'[46] There is clearly a step change from individual mental ill-health to a collective affliction, but there is a sliding scale of transition.

Some would say that the trend is more about anxiety than fear. Hence, it is important at the outset to distinguish the fine line between fear and anxiety. These emotions are closely related with both indicating the idea of danger or potential injury. One distinction is based on the premise that fear has a specific object whereas anxiety lacks this and is more general. Anxiety has a deeper level of concern.

The philosopher Immanuel Kant (d.1804) said that: 'Fear of an object that threatens with some indefinite evil is anxiety.'[47] The Norwegian philosopher Lars Svendsen in *The Philosophy of Fear* (2008) believes that fear tends to be 'deep' whereas anxiety is 'shallow'.[48] There is no doubt that fear can lead to anxiety and vice versa. The emphasis in this chapter will be on fear in its raw and direct form as it impacts resilience.

Whatever the distinction, both psychiatrists and physicians can offer a medical explanation of our fears. Studies in monkeys have shown that damage to a part of the brain normally involved in the regulation of emotions leads to a lack of fear, an increase in aggression or overreaction. A similar reaction has been recorded in people who have suffered damage through a tumour, for instance, to the amygdala—a pair of almond-shaped and -sized nerve clusters in the human brain. Such individuals can experience violent thoughts and actions as well as relationship problems. One woman patient with a damaged amygdala has been described as the 'woman with no fear'.[49]

The amygdala appear to be responsible for fear conditioning and our assessment of emotional events as well as the formation and storage of memories associated with those events. They play a pivotal role in controlling the state of fear. Interestingly, the size of the amygdala seems to correlate with both the number of contacts a person has and the number of social groups to which a person belongs.

The amygdala are also the primary structure of the brain responsible for the commonly recognised 'flight-or-fight' reaction to stressful situations. This is an automatic, physiological response associated with the activation of the sympathetic nervous system. It prepares the rest of the body—heart, circulation, lungs, liver, skin and eyes—for a quick response through the rapid release of the hormone adrenaline from the adrenal glands near the kidneys. The response is sometimes referred to as the 'defence cascade'. Many patients who suffer from anxiety disorders may have threat-response systems which have become over-active.

Similarly, patients with post-traumatic stress disorder (PTSD) may mistake the increased physiological arousal as an indicator that there is a genuine threat present. Understanding more about the flight-or-fight response can help people subdue their fears and enable them to feel more secure.

Resilience is thought to involve two other main regions of the human brain, namely the prefrontal cortex and the hippocampus. The former is involved in decision-making and emotional control. Activating this area is thought to improve the body's stress response and lead to greater psychological resilience. Research indicates that resilient people have greater connectivity between the prefrontal cortex, the hippocampus and amygdala, and when all are less stimulated.[50] There is also the role played by the neurotransmitter dopamine, released by the hypothalamus in the brain, which influences memory, movement, concentration and motivational salience[51]—all important elements in helping make a person resilient.

It is not surprising that commentators have tried to downplay the impacts of fear. "We have nothing to fear but fear itself," is an often-quoted line from Franklin D Roosevelt's first inaugural speech made after the 1932 presidential election in the USA. In full, he said: "So, first of all, let me assert my firm belief that the only thing we have to fear is…fear itself—nameless, unreasoning, unjustified terror which paralyses needed efforts to convert retreat into advance." The context in which Roosevelt made this speech was the Great Depression that America was plunged into following the Wall Street Crash (1929).

The gist of the address is that a 'positive mental attitude' will help to prevent the worst possible outcomes from materialising. It is worth noting, if only to indicate historical durability, that the sentiment that "we have nothing to fear except fear itself" originated with the French writer Michel de

Montaigne in the sixteenth century and was probably picked up by Francis Bacon in the seventeenth, before becoming a common proverb or axiom for later writers.[52]

In fact, the sentiment behind the overuse of the word fear goes back centuries. The first-century Roman philosopher Lucius Seneca the Younger (d.65) examined it in his correspondence with a young friend, later published as *Letters from a Stoic*.[53] In his thirteenth letter titled 'On Groundless Fears' (62), Seneca writes: 'There are more things…likely to frighten us than there are to crush us; we suffer more often in imagination than in reality.' [54]

With an eye to the self-defeating and wearying human habit of bracing ourselves for imaginary disaster, Seneca counsels his friend: 'What I advise you to do is, not to be unhappy before the crisis comes; since it may be that the dangers before which you paled as if they were threatening you, will never come upon you; they certainly have not yet come. Accordingly, some things torment us more than they ought; some torment us before they ought; and some torment us when they ought not to torment us at all. We are in the habit of exaggerating, or imagining, or anticipating, sorrow.'

Seneca then offers a critical assessment of both reasonable and unreasonable worries, using elegant rhetoric to illuminate the foolishness of squandering our mental and emotional energies on the latter class which comprises the vast majority of our anxieties: 'It is likely that some troubles will befall us; but it is not a present fact. How often has the unexpected happened! How often has the expected never come to pass! And even though it is ordained to be, what does it avail to run out to meet your suffering? You will suffer soon enough, when it arrives; so look forward meanwhile to better things.

What shall you gain by doing this? Time. There will be many happenings meanwhile which will serve to postpone, or end, or pass on to another person, the trials which are near or even in your very presence. A fire has opened the way to flight. Men have been let down softly by a catastrophe. Sometimes the sword has been checked even at the victim's throat. Men have survived their own executioners. Even bad fortune is fickle. Perhaps it will come, perhaps not; in the meantime, it is not. So, look forward to better things.'

Seneca recognised that hope is the great antidote to the 'culture of fear'. Resilience can help generate that hope as it offers the prospect of being able to overcome challenges and build back better; it offers a brighter future through the present gloom. Seneca encouraged us to: 'weigh carefully your hopes as well as your fears, and whenever all the elements are in doubt, decide in your own favour; believe what you prefer. And if fear wins a majority of the votes, incline in the other direction anyhow, and cease to harass your soul, reflecting continually that most mortals, even when no troubles are at hand or are expected in the future, become excited and disquieted.'

But the greatest peril of misplaced worry, Seneca cautions, is that keeping us constantly tensed against an imagined catastrophe prevents us from fully living. He encourages us to make the most of life's shortness and when loss does strike the key is resilience.

The German philosopher Hans Jonas (d.1993) advocated what he calls a 'heuristics of fear'.[55] Fear, he believed, has a moral imperative. This is not a fear that should degenerate into hopelessness but rather a fear that contains a hope that is within our power to avoid what is feared. The basic characteristic of Jonas's position is the precautionary principle where there is the potential for causing harm when extensive scientific knowledge on the matter is lacking.

We err on the side of caution: better to be safe than sorry. For example, a government may decide to limit or restrict the widespread release of a medicine or new technology until it has been thoroughly tested. The principle acknowledges that while the progress of science and technology has often brought great benefit to humanity, it has also contributed to the creation of new threats and risks. It implies that there is a social responsibility to protect the public from exposure to such harm when scientific investigation has found a plausible risk. These protections should be relaxed only if further scientific findings emerge that provide sound evidence that no harm will result.

The principle has gained broad recognition over the years in response to uncertainty and the need to act responsibly in the absence of proof. It has become an underlying rationale for a large and increasing number of international treaties and declarations in the fields of sustainable development, environmental protection, health, trade and food safety.[56] However, there are opponents. If we stipulate that precaution is required in the face of uncertain harms and precautionary measures also carry a risk of harm, the precautionary principle can both demand and prohibit action at the same time.

Loss and harm may be the result of a sudden catastrophe as much as a slow-burn stress. Shocks and stresses can be equal harbingers and generators of fear. The other fear is that of change. In general, people feel comfortable with their surroundings and routine. They give reassurance to the vagaries of life. While also wanting to better themselves, unless this is self-initiated then external pressures can be resisted. When threatened with new circumstances, people tend to retreat and fend off change. The solution to countering this fear is to develop a resilience mindset. Resilience expects failure but also anticipates a positive retort. This can come with help from the same source as the change if that help is acknowledged. It can also come from self-nurturing and maturation through training and experience.

While not an antidote, fear can have an upside in having an attractiveness to challenge the routineness of life and to push boundaries. Some like to read horror books and view scary films, albeit in the confines of a safe space. Others pursue extreme sports while recognising the dangers of injury or possible death. The rush of adrenaline in the face of the risks can be an aphrodisiac, enticing the participant to repeat or take ever more risks. Soldiers in battle can have a similar rush of exhilaration, especially when the situation is faced with comrades, and allows them to return to the fray again and again. Experience and training can also lower the fear threshold and allow those to achieve courageous or death-defying feats: some adopt the famous motto of the Special Air Service (SAS) 'Who Dares Wins'.

In a TED talk in 2017, Tim Ferriss recast the Stoic technique of pre-rehearsing evils as a way of dealing with hard choices that involve, as he described, what we most fear doing.[57] He called this technique 'fear setting', a replacement for goal setting. He breaks down the challenge into three components. The first is a list of fears in full detail, visualising the worst-case scenarios. The second is a corresponding list of what one can do to prevent the bad outcomes, again in full detail.

The third is a list of what damage repair looks like to prevent bad outcomes. In a nutshell, Ferriss believes it is about knowing the enemy one might be fighting, doing one's best to prevent the worst, and if prevention does not work focusing on the fixes. The Stoics called this 'dwelling in advance'. The approach places the emphasis on foresight, with a good measure of insight. As humans, unlike other creatures, we have a unique ability to dwell far into the future for better or worse. This has given rise to the idea of horizon-scanning which has developed into a sophisticated skill of forecasting.

Rather than placing a measurement on fear and fear setting, we have increasingly reverted to the word risk, an attribute that focuses more on the causes of the fear than the fear itself. For companies and governments alike, this shift goes against the Stoic principle by externalising the fear (under a different banner) and making it less personally emotional and more organisationally manageable. Risk and fear are the reverse sides of the same threat coin. It is important therefore to look more closely at this relationship if we are to face our fears.

Risk is seen as the combination of threat (harm) and vulnerability (weakness), with the capability of response sometimes added to the equation. Out of this has spawned a complex risk-management architecture with terms like risk awareness, risk avoidance, risk transfer, risk tolerance, risk appetite and risk capacity all becoming part of the management lexicon. In terms of measurement, impact (consequences) and likelihood (probability) are commonly used to assess risk on an individual case-by-case basis. A 5x5 matrix is often used to display graphically the assessed risks, with scales reflecting timeframes and seriousness.

As an example of a risk matrix, the National Risk Register is published by the UK government. Each risk identified is assessed on a 5x5 matrix by impact (scale 1–5 on the vertical axis) and likelihood (scale 1–5 on the horizontal axis). The 2023 and 2025 matrices each display eighty-nine risks in nine risk categories This marks an increase of 134 percent in the number of risks from the 2020 edition, contained within around a third more pages.

The risks range from the chances of assassination of a high-profile public figure to a major outbreak of African horse sickness. The highest risk is a pandemic while the lowest risk is an earthquake. All the risks are described against a reasonable worst-case scenario (RWCS). These scenarios represent the worst plausible manifestation of that particular risk—once highly unlikely variations have been discounted—to enable relevant bodies to undertake proportionate planning.

There are issues with this approach. First, probability is often measured in terms of historical precedent. However, a risk that may have occurred many times in the past may not necessarily reoccur in the same frequency in the future. The problem here is that many risks, especially those related to climate and health, are occurring increasingly often and with more intensity: flooding, for instance, is now so frequent in some areas that insurers will not indemnify the risks. If old probabilities no longer hold, new baselines need to be created against which relevant conclusions can be drawn going forward.

Second, and relatedly, risks have become more complex—as societies have become more complex—with interrelated issues setting off a cascade of effects that were perhaps unforeseen but have widespread impacts over a prolonged duration. We only have to consider the consequential nature of the loss of electrical power to realise that heating, communications, transport, sewerage, banking, medical, etc, would all be quickly affected.

In a wider context, a Chinese invasion of Taiwan, a mega-hub for chip manufacturing, would have repercussions way beyond the region in terms of disruption to the financial markets, international travel, shipping routes, supply chains, vehicle manufacture, etc. Even single incidents like the grounding of the *EverGiven* ship in the Suez Canal (2021) or the collision of the *Dali* ship in Baltimore harbour (2024) indicate the global repercussions of relatively small-scale accidents.

Third, the use of the term RWCS removes the extremes from the standard bell-curve probability distribution. This is not necessarily indicative of the most likely outcome. It is a subjective approach that can be misleading as it incorporates a degree of official bias and policy assumptions, not least of which is who determines what is reasonable or not. The assessment is often left to lead government departments. Take, for example, the UK's influenza pandemic scenario from the UK's National Risk Register of 2020. It was chosen on the basis of what was reasonable for the National Health Service to plan.

Yet, it is known that this was not the scenario that unfolded as COVID-19 turned out to be a non-influenza type pathogen and resulted in many more deaths than anticipated. The 2023 register thankfully has a generic pandemic scenario which should place a better level of preparedness for most manifestations of the risk.

The example given of a national risk register has introduced three terms related to likelihood—probability, possibility and plausibility. Frank Furedi in his book *How Fear Works* (2018) has suggested that a 'culture of fear' conflates possibility with probability (and plausibility) and is exemplified by the notion of 'zero risk' and a highly precautionary culture in which risk is invariably a negative factor.[58] The distinction between the three terms not only has semantic importance but also generates a better conception of what futures practice we could work towards.

In brief, probability refers to concepts of chance and likeliness. A probable future is more likely than some other future. Likeliness should mainly lead to the ordinal ranking of alternative futures between more likely and less likely e.g., 5–25 per cent. Whether we select more or fewer likely futures is a matter of investigation. Possibility, on the other hand, refers to a claim of reality whether some future can or cannot be with nothing in-between, e.g., yes or no. A possible future is considered by default to be potentially realisable, either passively or actively.

The possibility can be challenged for reasons such as violation of established laws or lack of realism with respect to the proposed timeframe or available means. When plausibility is introduced, it refers to the structure of the argument where value is based on the credibility of the description of the future. A plausible future is a convincing description of a future scenario which we can hold true even though the future itself can be factually fallacious. A future can be plausible without being possible.[59]

Possibility and probability are too often used interchangeably but incorrectly. Take this example: a college risk register might contain a strategic risk that the institution might be unable to attract the right calibre of academic staff. That is a distinct possibility (i.e., yes) but the probability for a good college is likely to be quite small (e.g., <5 per cent).

There is a danger that the more insecure and inward-looking we seemingly become in our modern society, the more we tend to indulge in the possibilities behind risks of today and tomorrow, with some dubious and time-consuming risk assessments resulting. Dr Chris Needham-Bennett believes that we should: 'maintain a strict focus on what might be termed "real risk" as the frivolous and vexatious risks have begun to be far too prevalent, risks bringing the discipline into disrepute as being little more than a prophylactic measure.'[60] The search generates an interesting paradox.

Needham-Bennett goes on to say that: 'Historical legacies of custom and practice seem to imbalance risk perceptions; "new things" are more risk managed. I can fill my car with an explosive, carcinogenic liquid at most out-of-town shopping centres; I can even leave my children in the car while I do it. I have had no training at all, and as far as I know, there is no course on how to do it. If, however, I take adult students on a geography field trip and wish to dig a shallow soil trench, I must complete a full risk assessment and wear the almost obligatory yellow personal protective equipment.' This shows the absurdity of some risk scaling.

Risk appetite and risk tolerance are defined and refined activities that play a key role in the approach of organisations to risk and the completion of corporately-required risk registers. Risk tolerance is the level of risk that an organisation is willing to accept per individual risk, whereas risk appetite is the total risk that the organisation can bear in pursuing its objectives over the longer term.

Risk appetite reflects the risk-management philosophy that an organisation wants to adopt and, in turn, influences its risk culture, operating style and decision-making. To take a motoring analogy: the designated speed limit on certain roads reflects the country's approach to road safety and its risk appetite; the allowable variance by any individual from that limit before incurring a fine is the risk tolerance.

Our modern culture does seem to have elevated overall risks to new heights and with it the fear quotient. Even if 'zero risk' places an unrealistic bar on our outlook, the common expectation is that every measure be taken (and recorded) in order to reduce the risks to a minimum. The litigious nature of relationships, as well as stringent health and safety regimes, in the pursuit of wrongful actions, is a strong incentive for good risk management.

This attitude can, however, stifle innovation and risk-taking while generating additional legislation and regulation. It has also produced a rush to introduce standards of various natures to ensure interoperability and safety. These can be tickbox exercises, overly complex and pedantic, while not ensuring scalability (for all organisations) but with shortcuts incorporated. They can become no more than certificates displayed on walls for some.

Fear and risk, restless bedfellows, are on the increase. After the Cold War, the Western world believed that widening and deepening commercial ties would make the world safer. Yet, as the global economy has become vastly more complex, and geopolitical tensions have increased, it has instead become more fraught. This has made it more difficult to understand while our ability to manage it has eroded. The risks have escalated and the corresponding fears have encouraged populations to look for seemingly safe havens or at least vote for leaders who purport to be able to generate them.

Regrettably, some leaders feel that by deliberately exaggerating or weaponising the fears and their proffered solutions, they will be more able to control their populations. This allows them to introduce even more security measures which in themselves raise the fear levels further.

As a result, we are witnessing more populist and xenophobic politicians, some of whom favour autocracies. Tensions rise and Manichean divisions (a binary bias) multiply. Conflicts are mushrooming, with savagery and death prevalent in many. According to data provided by the Uppsala Conflict Data Program, the number, intensity and length of conflicts worldwide is at its highest level since before the end of the Cold War. The data indicated that there were fifty-five active conflicts in 2022, with an average duration of eight to eleven years, a substantial increase from the thirty-three active conflicts lasting an average of seven years a decade earlier.

Moreover, a quarter of the world's population—two billion people—lived in conflict-affected areas in 2022. The overall trend may be towards what the American historian Samuel Huntington called *A Clash of Civilizations* (1997).[61] We as a human race face existential risks for which we have every reason to be fearful unless politicians act for the benefit and saviour of the whole of humanity. The runes are not good. Talk of an 'unravelling' of traditional social, political, and even environmental, order is discernible and gaining volume. Some have referred to this period as the 'great alignment' and believe it is driven by both geopolitical competition and localisation in politics.[62]

Decoupling and derisking, with 'zero-sum' trade-offs between risk and rewards, rather than interdependence are the vogue and favoured policies of many countries. Yet, as Anthea Roberts, founder of Dragonfly Thinking, wrote in *Foreign Affairs* (2023): 'Companies and countries need to embed calculations about risk and reward in a broader framework of systemic resilience—that is, the characteristics of a system that determine its ability to survive and thrive over time. Although resilience is commonly understood as the ability to withstand shocks and stressors, it is about more than just effectively responding to risks. It is also about evolving to better capture future rewards and cope with change.'[63] She continued to say that if we always aim to minimise risks, we will also reduce the rewards while creating new vulnerabilities.

We can only face the fears and risks through good political leadership and systemic resilience based on a sound understanding of ourselves and the ways of implementing better global governance. The proactive bonding of communities and engagement of whole sections of society will allow faster recovery from any pending disaster. Those systemic disasters or unknowns will also require us to be adaptive if we are to manage our fears.

Chapter 4
Realising Our Virtues

The superior man thinks always of virtue; the common man thinks of comfort.

– **Confucius**

A virtue is a quality or a trait that acts as a foundational principle because it is both a morally good thing and an inner strength conferred on the pursuant. It should be a quotidian objective that is relevant no matter what changes may be taking place around; this makes it powerful and constant. The Stoics believed that when we acted virtuously, we were pursuing a path towards a good life, a journey of 'moral excellence'. A person who is virtuous therefore avoids doing what is wrong and strives to do what is right. Virtue lies between knowledge and action. The goal of achieving perfect consistency to be virtuous was a life-long task that was both important and possible but demanded determination and courage to achieve. The task remains a tall order!

Modern virtue ethics were popularised during the late twentieth century through the re-examination of the thinking of the early Stoics. At the turn of the twentieth century, moral theories became more complex and were no longer concerned solely with rightness and wrongness but were interested in many kinds of moral status. As a result, philosophers began to think of virtue ethics in terms of how people should act (normative ethics) and what people think is right (descriptive ethics). In the modern world of work, virtue ethics represent those behaviours that any individual or group should exhibit within an organisation that can affect the business's core values.

It must be acknowledged from the outset that different religions and cultures have different virtues. For example, Christianity has described seven heavenly virtues: chastity, temperance, charity, diligence, patience, kindness and humility. The 'Four Faces of the Heart' in Buddhism can also be viewed as virtues: loving kindness, compassion, altruistic joy and equanimity.

On the other hand, the Chinese philosophy of Taoism is based on three pillars or 'jewels', loosely translated as compassion, frugality and humility.[64] Lao-Tzu, the founder of Taoism (c.500 BC), wrote in the 'The Way of Virtue' (*Tao-TeChing*) that these three virtues were our greatest treasures. A common goal of Taoist practice is self-cultivation and a more harmonious existence. Concepts like Taoism highlight the idea of effortless action and spontaneity, suggesting that being in harmony with the flow of life requires agility and adaptation.

In his book *The Republic (*c.375 BC*)*, Plato outlined four cardinal virtues—wisdom, courage, moderation and justice—which he believed constituted unity.[65] It meant that if you had one of these virtues, you had them all and will be wise, brave, temperate and fair. Seneca, the Roman Stoic, believed that a prudent person would act in a way that is indistinguishable from a virtuous person because a prudent person considers all consequences. Plato echoed this belief as he said that people make bad choices instead of prudent ones due to a lack of wisdom.

These attributes articulated millennia ago have resonance today.[66] The classical virtues are tools to help us grow to be more resilient. When we face challenges, we can draw on these virtues to guide our actions and help us navigate difficult situations and bounce forward. For example, if we encounter a setback in our professional life, we can draw on our courage to persevere through the challenge and find a solution. If we are dealing with a difficult relationship, we can practise justice by treating the other person with kindness and respect even if we disagree with them. And if we are facing a health issue, we can apply moderation and patience by looking after our well-being (body and mind) and by focusing on self-preservation and mindfulness.

Of the four virtues, wisdom is often considered the principal one. In more modern times, Dr Rasmi Parmar, a psychiatrist, believes that it is possible to understand wisdom through a three-dimensional model based on cognition, reflection and compassion.[67] The cognitive dimension refers to a person's need to understand the deeper truths of life including its positive and negative aspects. The reflective dimension paves the way to this understanding by pondering events from many perspectives rather than blaming others or circumstances. The compassionate dimension brings a broad awareness of human nature and suffering that motivates people to help others with sympathy and compassion.

Parmar writes that: 'the reflective dimension has an especially strong effect on a person's well-being: in short, reflective wisdom allows people to understand and, more importantly, accept their reality.' The American psychiatrist Theodore Rubin takes the view that: 'Kindness is more important than wisdom and the recognition of this is the beginning of wisdom.'[68]

While much more has and no doubt will be written about wisdom, for the purpose of this philosophical journey on resilience the focus will be on three aspects, namely hindsight (experience), insight (knowledge) and foresight (awareness). As the Irish blessing advises us: 'May you have the hindsight to know where you've been, the foresight to know where you are going, and the insight to know when you have gone too far.' This guidance echoes the Stoic philosophy of controlling how we respond to external events rather than being controlled by them.

The listed attributes are not the only ones, or may not be even the most influential, but they are convenient hooks on which to hang a discussion of the subject of wisdom with the intention of identifying how we can best apply ourselves to become more resilient. One definition of resilience is the ability to 'Anticipate, Absorb and Adapt' to change.[59] (Some believe that if there is dramatic change, transformation is a better word than adaptation which infers incremental adjustments: the latter will be used here to signify both.)

The three 'A's loosely correspond to the words foresight, hindsight and insight respectively. This analysis of wisdom will precede an examination of the other virtues listed of moderation, courage and justice, before taking a separate look at values.

Foresight is about envisioning a probable or possible future in the medium to longer term rather than a shorter timeframe and, importantly, preparing for it. Two ideasare crucial here, namely vision and preparation. The first is not a prediction but a willingness and capacity to peer beyond the immediate and seriously contemplate what actions will be necessary to overcome the anticipated challenges and be resilient—to survive and thrive. It is about identifying a 'north star', one that will set the course for the journey ahead. The second idea is about being proactive rather than purely reactive when facing challenges. Such a mindset applies to all manner of resilience characteristics, from leadership to resourcing.

Without preparation, vision is a vacant vessel. As the adage warns: 'to be prepared is to be forearmed'. Yet, preparation is more than a set of plans in response to being situationally aware. Preparation involves having a strategy for coping with stresses and shocks—a resilience strategy that, like all good strategies, sets out in detail how to maintain 'a balance between ends, ways, and means; about identifying objectives; and about the resources and methods available for meeting such objectives.'[70]

This is the definition of strategy offered by the British academic Sir Lawrence Freedman in his book *Strategy* (2013). He states that: 'Having a strategy suggests an ability to look up from the short term and the trivial to view the long term and the essential, to address causes rather than symptoms, to see woods rather than trees. Without a strategy, facing up to any problem or striving for any objective would be considered negligent.' The timeframe for a strategy depends on horizon-scanning capabilities to identify challenges and priorities.

Preparation as part of a resilience strategy can also deter potentially harmful actions. By showing an opponent that one can withstand and recover from an assault, to weather the storm, it may deflect that opponent from attacking in the first instance. Clearly, if deterrence is to be effective by being believed by the opponent, it needs to be real and active with resources to support the case. A weak resilience strategy, one that fails to have preparatory responses across the panoply of possible threats not just one or two, may be insufficient for a serious opponent to test the waters.

They say hindsight is about having a perception of the past through rose-tinted spectacles. It is about being wise after the event, ideally with the precision of twenty-twenty vision. The truth is that events often seem more obvious and predictable after they have already happened but not at the time. While one might have been able to guess at the outcome before the event, such a prediction is just that.

It certainly does not prevent comments such as 'I knew it all along', a clear case of hindsight bias. Yet, within this unrealistic post-event acuity, there is a modicum of valuable assessment that is about looking at past events and understanding what practices were good or bad, with the aim of emphasising the good and avoiding the bad for next time.

This appraisal is helped by two related characteristics, one is experience and the other is learning. It is common to associate experience (and resilience) with age and life skills. The greater awareness and involvement that a person may have of varied challenges and the ways of rising above them allows a broader and more balanced perspective to be taken in the cold light of day: it is the reflective dimension described by Dr Parmar.

Being more aware of feelings and having the ability to exert greater control over negative emotions, especially those who seek to blame others, make for a heightened perspective. It is therefore understandable why more mature people have the experience and skills to accept reality and show a good degree of hindsight. However, younger people cannot be excluded from the calculation. Sometimes, younger people can show remarkable hindsight by having greater awareness and perspicacity of their situation and others around them, as well as quickly picking up on the experiences of friends and colleagues. It is better to avoid mistakes by learning from the errors of others if the willingness to absorb is present.

Learning lessons, that other aspect of hindsight, is much acknowledged but often easier said than done. It is truly a case of wisdom, if not duty, to avoid the errors of the past. The physicist Albert Einstein is reportedly (although mistakenly) to have said that: 'The definition of insanity is doing the same thing over and over again and expecting a different result.' While this is a recognised human failing, there is human strength in that more often than not we do manage to learn from past failures or omissions to improve the future. Learning can help build an adaptive capacity—hence resilience—to respond to novel threats. (Learning is discussed in *Chapter 8.*)

All too often, inquiries and post-incident reports are greeted with the refrain that mistakes have been acknowledged and lessons will be learnt. Translating lessons through a learning process into meaningful actions, however, is sometimes difficult and painful, and often requires imagination and transformation. In fact, a failure of imagination is a frequent refrain in post-incident reporting. It was one of four reasons clearly stated by the *9/11 Commission Report* (2004), together with 'a mindset that dismissed possibilities'.[71] This is why it is important to have a system in place that records and transfers lessons—in effect, contributes to the corporate memory of an organisation. With the churn in some organisations, having a repository to which new employees can turn by way of induction and from which they can learn what pitfalls to avoid is worth its weight in gold.

Besides a lack of imagination, there is a myriad of other reasons for the chasm between learning and application. This includes: misunderstanding, misappreciation, fear of the consequences, loss aversion, paralysis in decision-making, groupthink (the downside of collective decision-making), prejudice or bias in the processing, bureaucratic inertia because of departmental silos, concern about undermining communities, too little or too much information, or a reluctance to release funding. There are many examples of each of these in the crisis-management literature. We will consider some of the solutions in the following chapters.

If hindsight is about looking backwards, insight is about looking forwards. It is not fighting the same wars of the past but finding ways to fight the next one in new ways. As the Anglo-Irish statesman and philosopher Edmund Burke (d.1797) wrote: 'You can never plan the future by the past.'[72] But, to refine the Stoic argument, we should avoid staggering backwards into the future seeing only where we have come from.

Insight is the capacity to gain an accurate and deep understanding of a situation for future benefit. It is not a simple observation or in-depth statement but rather a fundamental truth that reveals the inner nature of things that gives rise to a re-examination of existing conventions and proposes, when required, a new *status quo*. It is a fresh perspective of motivations and momentum. Such constructive challenge enables decision-makers to avoid decision bias or groupthink through a process based on logic, evidence, consequence analysis, alternative perspectives and the competitive environment.

Such insight and re-evaluation make it possible to adapt to a new situation more readily. It allows new opportunities to be grasped. Adaptability reflects that sweet spot between reaction and anticipation, providing an ability to respond efficiently to a wide range of potential challenges, not just those that are known or scoped. (Adaptability is explored further in *Chapter 7.*)

Having looked in detail at wisdom, attention is now directed to the second named virtue, that of courage. Courage and resilience are worthy compatriots. Both attract descriptive words like tenacity, fortitude, mettle and spirit. They are about doing the right thing in the face of adversity and having the determination and confidence to step into the unknown and tackle the hurdles in front. The element of fear and anxiety is there to be overcome. Nassim Taleb makes a valid point in his book *Skin in the Game* (2018) that: 'Courage is the only virtue you cannot fake.'[73]

Courage comes in many forms: essentially, there is both physical courage and psychological (mental and moral) courage. The two are inextricably linked. Often, they combine in an outpouring of supreme acts of heroism or bravery in difficult and dangerous situations. At other times, they manifest themselves separately in less dramatic fashion but are not diminished by so doing.

In more routine circumstances, courage and resilience reflect a strength of character that shines through the gloom.

It requires endurance, high-mindedness and cheerfulness. It can be infectious and others will willingly follow, even in the face of possible death. Courage can certainly be enhanced with training and experience, but beneath the surface, it must be accompanied by a set of values or morals that help drive the human spirit and is central to a person's identity. One of the most common acts of courage we see is when someone stands up for what they believe and their core values. Yet crises can produce grey areas where previously held values and certainties can be challenged—fighting in a war is an example of the sacrilege of killing in peacetime.

Some psychologists refer to courage as 'ego strength'. This includes self-confidence but is broader as it means having a sense of one's self, having a sense of purpose and determination to succeed, while being independent of other people for approval or survival. Those linked qualities are essential for exploring new solutions and overcoming fear in a crisis. They are said to arise in childhood but are not necessarily genetic traits. Some people with difficult upbringings have also shone through and have become very resilient characters.

A sure way to exercise courage and resilience daily is by facing challenges head-on. While easier said than done, if practised consistently it reinforces the message that the owner has what it takes to overcome obstacles and achieve success. When the difficulties are avoided or the *status quo* goes unchallenged, not only may the growth opportunities be missed but also the chance to set an example and demonstrate courage to others may be lost.

The third cardinal virtue is moderation or temperance. This has to do with our ability to practise self-control, to act modestly and to be prudent in our actions. It includes aspects of our own well-being in the face of life's stresses and strains. Seneca said that: 'Everything that exceeds the bounds of moderation has an unstable foundation.' This may seem old-fashioned in today's world when excess is all around, at least in the hands of some, but shines through in our collective efforts to show proportionality and sustainability. It reflects trying to stay on the centre ground and keep cool heads when 'all around are losing theirs' as Rudyard Kipling wrote in his famous poem '*If*'.[74]

Resilience is about surviving and thriving for the long term, and this can only be achieved if we find paths that appeal to the common sense of the majority. In democracies, politicians recognise that this is where elections are won, and hence where power belongs. We are constantly pulled to the extremes by minorities and, as we shall see, this has its own resilience when the ground around is unstable but one that is not likely to win over most of the people for most of the time.

Proportionality, a form of moderation, applies in times of both war and peacetime. It is one of those key elements that Saints Augustine (d.430) and Thomas Aquinas (d.1274) used to define a just war. The former is considered to be the last great philosopher of Latin antiquity while the latter's philosophy (Thomism) bridged the gap between Christianity and Aristotelian thinking.

By their interpretations, people seeking war should justify their response in proportion to the claimed wrong (*jus ad bellum*) while the means used to carry out that war should be proportionate to the desired goal (*jus in bello*). Acting disproportionally is morally reprehensible and likely to lead to an escalation of revenge and extremism. To be morally legitimate, war also requires a realistic chance of restoring what has been unjustly seized. The Roman statesman and philosopher Marcus Cicero (d.43 BC) argued that there was only one justification for going to war and that was to live 'peaceably without suffering injustice'.

While wars in the Greco-Roman period were perhaps more clearly delineated, in the modern era they are less so, particularly with acts of both terrorism and hybrid warfare on the rise. There are fewer discernible lines here: one man's terrorist is another man's freedom fighter illustrates the point. In fact, the terrorist attacks of 9/11 have, through a so-called 'war on terrorism', unleashed a derogation of justice as all types of responses are considered permissible.

Polarisation of political affairs, stretching into extremism, may be unwelcomed but their proponents do generate resilience by virtue of their ingrained ardour. They have a tremendous capacity to survive and perpetuate their ideology and show resilience in the face of legal and official challenges. There is no reason to indicate from past trends that their resilience will falter in the future. In fact, we can expect 'resilience of the extremes' to continue and indeed flourish as the fragmentation of ideas and the division of political parties offer them space to develop. Proportionality displayed by extremist groups may be one feature that does not hold up. Yet, states can also be guilty.

In peacetime, proportionality can be viewed through the prism of seeking ever more growth and riches in a world that has finite resources. We have certainly been successful so far, with eight billion people currently inhabiting the earth, while the number is expected to reach ten billion by the end of this century. Humans now dominate the planet to such an extent that together we weigh more than ten times that of all the wild animals on the land combined: three hundred and ninety million tonnes versus twenty-two million tonnes respectively.[75] Success in numbers has brought about its own problems, however, one of which is the need for around 80 per cent more earth equivalents to sustain the human population if we continue to consume the world's resources at the present rate.[76]

We simply cannot continue to seek sustainable growth on a linear trajectory without accelerating our overall destruction of the planet. We need to find ways to be more resilient by conserving what exists and making more efficient use of it. One of many approaches proposed is the 'degrowth' theory and movement.[77] It argues that economic growth measured by GDP should be abandoned as a policy objective. Instead, policy should focus on economic and social metrics such as life expectancy, health, education, housing, and ecologically sustainable work as indicators of both ecosystems and human well-being. The Stoics would argue that ethical thinking and actions should pervade in the pursuance of all growth.

There is a philosophy and religious fervour which promotes the 'benediction of enough'. This is commonly referred to as sustainability. It is important to distinguish between sustainability and resilience as the two concepts are related but not interchangeable. Sustainability is the capacity of an entire system to endure for a protracted period. In ecology, the word is used to describe how biological systems remain diverse and productive over time. Long-lived and healthy wetlands and forests are examples of sustainable ecosystems.

For humans, sustainability is the potential for long-term maintenance of well-being which has environmental, economic and social dimensions. Hence, a sustainable community can maintain the quality of life of its inhabitants over time from external pressures and from internal influences such as demographic change. As Alastair McAslan has pointed out: 'in a sustainable community, external pressures and internal influences are usually incremental, whereas a resilient community is able to cope in the face of adversity—to recover after confronting an abnormal, alarming and often unexpected threat. Communities can be both sustainable and resilient.' [78]

Another aspect of moderation and balance concerns risk and reward. Anthea Roberts has remarked: 'To thrive over the long term, systems need to find a middle ground between efficiency and resilience and between the desire to minimise risks and maximise rewards. Countries that aim to minimise risks in the short term often leave themselves vulnerable to long-term threats. Likewise, countries that aim to maximise short-term rewards often make themselves vulnerable to future shocks.'[79] She continues: 'So what is the right balance between peril and payoff? Where high risks promise high rewards, countries should abide by a simple rule: run the risk only when the relevant system has sufficient resilience to absorb, adapt or transform if that risk becomes reality.'

A balance has also to be achieved between reliability and performance in an effort to become resilient. Consider the FI racing car. Motor-racing engineers are constantly trying to make cars lighter by reducing any excess weight from the car's construction. The hope is that it will go faster and hence be more likely to win the race with the right driver. However, there is a balance here between removing that extra weight and ensuring that it does not compromise a critical part of the car and result in race failure or a crash. Judging between efficiency (reliability), risk (safety), and winning (performance) is a fine one in motor-racing.

That is true for other activities and getting the balance right can be difficult. As resilience increasingly comes into the equation, reliability is beginning to trump performance. This influences redundancy which is about incorporating surpluses in both systems and processes so that one is not caught short in any disruption. There will be constant questions about the cost-gain ratio of redundancy and efficiency depending on the volatility of the environment. In the words of Anthea Roberts: 'Whereas optimising for efficiency can create too many risks, optimising for resilience can generate too few rewards.'[80]

The scholar and former management consultant Roger Martin believes that the pursuit of all resilience and no efficiency is as problematic as the pursuit of efficiency with no resilience.[81]

Let us turn to the final virtue, that of justice or fairness. The good life, as conceived by Aristotle and contemporary thinkers, required more than moral, intellectual and personal virtues. It also centred on rights and responsibilities, how we act in relation to our fellow man, to the people in our community, and to our community as a whole. To Stoics, justice was not only something to be performed through the legal system but also, in a broader sense, one's duty to our society and to people around us. Seneca proclaimed that: 'It is a denial of justice not to stretch out a helping hand to the fallen that is the common right of humanity.' This interpretation has perhaps slipped in the modern concepts of justice but the wider view will be taken here.

On a global scale, it seems as if the international order and the justice that underpins it are breaking down. Traditional global institutions like the UN, the World Bank and the IMF are all struggling to apply their rules and edicts in an increasingly fractious and turbulent world. The end of the bipolar Cold War has given rise, after two decades, to today's Cold War 2.0 in which polarity is increasingly reflected in a struggle between authoritarian and democratic countries. According to the *Bertelsmann Stiftung's Transformation Index* (2024), out of one hundred and thirty-seven countries, only sixty-three remain democracies while a majority are classified as autocracies.[82]

Potential agreements at the UN Security Council over, say, Palestine are stymied by one veto while European Union Council agreements, on migration for example, are hampered by unanimous voting. Even when UN resolutions are based on agreed international laws, countries choose to violate them with relative impunity. In modern wars, the Geneva Conventions specifying the non-targeting civilians seem also to be casually ignored.

These actions not only undermine international justice but also lower the threshold of resilience. It is harder for people to bounce back from disruption if the framework for fairness and justice is unavailable or flaunted. In an ever more volatile and violent world, the argument for more collective (global) governance not less is powerful. This could be realised through serious revisions to organisations like the G7 or through the launch of new bodies like the D-10 Strategy Forum or President Macron's European Forum initiative.

In effect, these are 'coalitions of the willing' which could be referred to as global or single-issue networks. 'As malign actors try to undermine multilateral organisations', a former UK Foreign Secretary and later Prime Minister (Liz Truss) has spoken of the need for a 'new approach that builds stronger global alliances'.

Such networks may increasingly arise at the ground level but have a national or global impact on justice and fairness. Take the 'MeToo' movement which has had significance on the issue of sexual harassment and sexual abuse of women in the workplace since its inception in 2006. Then there is the 'Black Lives Matter' movement or the 'Iranian Democracy Movement' against the compulsory wearing of headscarves (*hijab*) or the 'Arab Spring' in 2010 which has since faltered. These are indicators of groundswell reactions to what are commonly perceived as injustices and oppression. As traditional political parties fragment, such reactions can be expected to increase.

Injustices can also be seen through the inequalities of wealth, race and sexual orientation around the globe. Take the Gini coefficient which is a measure of the distribution of income across a population. During the nineteenth and most of the twentieth centuries, global inequality increased dramatically, reflecting widening disparities between per capita income as advanced economies took off sharply compared with the rest of the world. The coefficient started to improve in the 1990s and did so for around three decades.[83] The World Bank estimates that seven hundred million people lived on less than US$2.15 a day in 2019, down from two billion in 1990.[84]

However, largely because of the COVID-19 pandemic, inequality may be on the rise again and returning to the levels of the early 2010s.[85] The European Union believes that more than 70 per cent of the global population lives in countries where the gap between rich and poor has widened over the last 30 years.[86] Others contest this finding and believe income inequality continues to fall in certain countries with a growing global middle class.[87] Whatever the actuality, a *Credit Suisse Global Wealth Report* in 2022 found that the world's richest 1 per cent, namely those with more than $1 million, owned 45.8 per cent of all the world's wealth.[88]

This inequality is a serious hindrance to making communities and populations more resilient because efforts are overly focused on those who have assets to protect and can arrange insurance rather than the betterment of the whole of society.

Consider the enrichment of two particular countries—India and China—that are home to more than a third of the world's population. While these nations are undoubtedly the big economic success stories of the past four decades, they have made slow progress for those at the lower end of the income spectrum. These people are more likely to live in areas that have poor sanitation (promoting disease), are subject to extreme weather events (destroying dwellings), occupy land that is less fertile (relying on aid) and are unlikely to afford insurance (to compensate for losses). The justice or fairness here is absent for millions.

In this debate, it should be acknowledged that high levels of social vulnerability because of poverty do not automatically indicate low levels of resilience. Even very vulnerable communities can be well organised and can possess significant social and cultural capital, with close-knit community ties, active support networks and vibrant community institutions such as churches.[89]

As well as direct legislation, regulation and the introduction of standards are two other ways of enhancing resilience. The relaxation of competition law in certain circumstances, for example, could allow competitors to collaborate ahead of a crisis, not just after the event. Pooling intelligence in areas of common concern would be beneficial as would sharing of mutually-beneficial lessons from past incidences. It is disappointing that the UK government has withdrawn legislation to allow the introduction of a Resilience Statement as part of the annual reporting by all large organisations.

Nevertheless, plans to codify the statement within corporate governance rules would help to make company boards take resilience more seriously, and non-executive directors would become ardent proponents of resilience principles such as stewardship and regulation. [90] The intentions will help drive efforts to measure resilience so that meaningful, if not absolute, assessments could be made of improvements and maturity advanced.

The regulation of artificial intelligence is an example of a wider question about the national appetite for impacts that society is willing to tolerate. While it is hard politically to make decisions on behalf of the whole of society, a first step is to be transparent about responsibilities and expected responses to crises. Service standards for critical infrastructures could help enable that. We must also be aware of the danger that if regulation is too tight around safety for instance, then innovation may be stifled.

Finally, one of the challenges of applying the virtues perspective is the measure of success in the context of resilience in any meaningful way. There has been little work done in this area that presents broad-based conclusions. One group of researchers tried in 2017 to do this for chronic illness and disability. In their report, resilience is defined as a positive by-product of having endured adversities while transforming them into insightful opportunities for renewal. The doctors introduced what they called a Virtue-based Psycho-social Adaptation Model (V-PAM) to determine its applicability to the study of resilience for the rehabilitation counselling of individuals.[91]

The five virtues addressed were: courage, integrity, practical wisdom, committed action, and emotional transcendence (i.e., meaning and hope). The overall findings from 256 college students were that each of the chosen virtues is highly relevant for resilience within the context of rehabilitation for chronic illnesses such as post-traumatic stress. Specifically, committed action was the strongest contributor to resilience, followed by emotional transcendence, practical wisdom, courage and integrity in that order.

Other research on other individuals and their particular circumstances may well reveal different conclusions. Nonetheless, the field is ripe for exploration and could help in training programmes that were designed to identify and then strengthen key characteristics around the classical virtues.

Chapter 5
Finding Our Values

A people that values its privileges above its principles soon loses both.
— **Dwight D Eisenhower**

Today, we rarely speak about virtues but prefer to use the word values, both in personal and professional contexts. This often results in the latter mirroring some of the characteristics of the former. Yet, the words virtue and value have very different connotations, and it is important to understand the nuances if we are to advance the discussion of the resilience mindset. Any distinction is not helped by the fact that people have different interpretations of values, as with virtues, and place different priorities according to their beliefs, customs and cultures. Both virtues and values tend not to change quickly but influence attitudes and behaviours over time.

If virtues are core qualities that are generally considered to be morally good and desirable, values are achieved through the consistent practice of virtue. Value can be viewed as what one believes to be important—goals, ideals or even opinions. It is a principle or standard of behaviour, often subjective and personal, that can help one to decide what is important in life.

In other words, values are lived and acted upon whereas virtues are experienced and observed.

To illustrate the point, take this simple example: scoring goals in a football match might be considered an important value to the team but if a player is unable to score because of a lack of knowledge of the game or a lack of courage—appropriate virtues—then value is diminished. At the same time, while wisdom is a worthy virtue, if creativity is inhibited or poor judgement exercised as values, such as displaying bad behaviour off the field, it is impossible for a player to be seen as truly wise. Values have a direct bearing on resilience and the degree to which people set their sights on any recovery and recuperation when a crisis occurs. Values are one of the factors that affect behaviours and influence the choices people make.

Once again, the ancient Greeks offer a foundation for the study of values under the theme of ethics. Socrates, Plato and Aristotle attempted to provide a rational response to the question of how humans should best live. Aristotle argued that the man who possessed moral excellence would tend to do the right thing at the right time and in the right way, and the highest aim was living well (*eudaimonia*).[92] The Stoic philosopher Epictetus believed that the greatest good was contentment and serenity, and peace of mind (*apatheia*) was of the highest value.

European philosophers such as the German Friedrich Nietzsche (d.1900) and Frenchman Jean-Paul Sartre (d.1980) were key figures in the concept of existentialism which holds that we are each responsible for creating purpose or meaning in our own lives. Nietzsche explored the idea of overcoming difficulties and embracing challenges as a way of personal growth. He believed that life was ultimately a struggle but within which we can find hope and meaning. 'We strive to find meaning in the teeth of mortality; we strive to co-operate harmoniously in the teeth of selfishness' is how the commentator Matthew Syed expresses the struggle. [93] Nietzsche's famous phrase 'what does not kill me makes me stronger' resonates with the idea of resilience.

Nietzsche questioned the morals and values of the ancient Greeks, as well as those of the subsequent Judaeo-Christian period, and believed that we should search for new values more akin to our modern age and divorced from religious beliefs. These values must be based on ourselves, and we are free to choose whatever values it is most in our own interests to have such as imagination, strength, bravery and daring. Acceptance of these values can release our creative potential and provide great self-fulfilment. Nietzsche's idea of 'will to power' (i.e., the source of a person's strength) has echoes of the Stoic ideals of confronting challenges.

Sartre's existentialist philosophy also encouraged individuals to take responsibility for their choices and find meaning in the face of life's challenges. This existential responsibility can contribute to a resilient mindset at least on a personal level. Yet, the question that both philosophers struggled to address was how individual values contribute to wider social resilience as they could make living together harmoniously rather problematic. Some would argue that focusing on one's own values, regardless of the consequences, contributed to the odious political regimes in the 1930s. Nietzsche's name is often linked, perhaps unfairly, to such regimes.

When contemplating ethical values, it is important to differentiate between personal, social and professional ones. Personal values stem from a culture, largely arising from home and family, that shares a set of common values based on an understanding of what has been taught as right and wrong. They can include attributes such as honesty, generosity, kindness, tolerance, respect and trustworthiness. (Trust and truth are examined in *Chapter 6.*)

Many of these values would also apply to communities and social groups but with the emphasis shifting to wider values such as cooperation, civility, charity, integrity, accountability and loyalty. This is where, contrary to philosophers like Nietzsche, it is necessary to turn from inward to outward values and see the cultivation of a healthy society and its values overriding self-assertion and the belief in the power of the strong usurping the weak.

As for professional and commercial values, these can be a set of guiding principles that determine how an organised body wishes to conduct its business. Beyond fulfilling legal obligations, ethical values here are reflected in the positive moral character exhibited by leaders and employees alike. They include attributes such as innovation, leadership, empowerment, reliability, equality, safety, transparency, value for money and customer focus. They are often cited in company literature without much thought given to their significance or application to stakeholders and the wider public.

If business values are what a company will deliver, ethical values are how those business values will be achieved. Ethical values guide the way that activities are conducted; they specify what is considered acceptable or desirable behaviour, above and beyond compliance with laws and regulations. They provide purpose and direction and set the tone for interactions with customers, employees and other parties. They offer a moral compass, both personal and professional, by which all should be judged uniformly and consistently.

In his book *Upheaval: How Nations cope with Crisis and Change* (2019), Jared Diamond makes the important point that while some personal core values overlap with national core values, integrity being one such cross-over, national values are not necessarily identical to national identities.[94] He cites the example of 'the language of Shakespeare [being] part of Britain's national identity' but not part of the national value of 'never surrender' during wartime. Diamond also draws attention to the fact that while values may help to resolve a crisis by providing clarity and certainty, they can also become traps if they prevent flexibility in changed circumstances. Values should not be immutable but rather guides to a better future.

Before delving further into such values, it is necessary to consider the purpose of an organisation in more depth as purpose is fundamental to value setting. If a vision statement describes what the long-term aspirations and ambitions of an organisation are, the purpose is about why it is on that particular journey and what opportunities it is seeking to realise. An illustration could be for a vision to be the 'most resilient company in the market' while a purpose could be 'to generate a sustainable future by building back better after and between any disruptions (whether from shocks or stresses) while benefiting shareholders, stakeholders and the environment.' Purpose defines goals and establishes a route map; it provides that lodestar by which to guide the ship. It also shapes core principles and values which, in turn, help cement corporate culture.[95] It is the essence of a business-oriented philosophy.

Purpose has traditionally been focused on shareholder value, with profit margins and internal benefits as primary if not sole drivers. In resilience it is necessary to rephrase—even transform—this notion by looking more towards the long-term effects on people, customers, markets, investors, the wider community and the natural environment. In other words, it should adopt what has become known as a 'whole-of-society approach' in an effort to make an organisation more resilient and sustainable. Purpose should show how society at large will benefit from the organisation's existence. By way of an example, Unilever's purpose of 'making sustainable living commonplace' has been rephrased into a core aim of 'doubling the size of the business through strong performance while decoupling environmental impact from that growth, and optimising the company's social impact'.

Purpose-driven organisations (now defined by the Publicly Available Specification (PAS) 808:2022)[96] should offer a clear, common focus applicable across the whole organisation, one that helps to engage and motivate employees, and prioritises competing demands. It also helps people feel personally and emotionally invested in the organisation and allows them to watch, whether individually or collectively, for changes in the business and the wider market, and be empowered to act.

According to Roz Brewer, chief executive of Walgreen Boots Alliance in 2023, 80 per cent of firms united by a common purpose were found to outperform the general market, while 65 per cent of candidates said they would accept a job offer only if they knew and agreed with a company's purpose, vision and values.[97] Brewer has called for a 'rephrasing of the corporate environment'…'Just as sentences must sometimes be rephrased for greater effect, so must companies.' Brewer means by this that we 'approach our work in a different way that has clearer meaning'. The rephrasing can help improve resilience by improving our ability to respond and adapt.

The idea of profit with purpose, or at least social purpose, is behind the notion of stakeholder capitalism. An influential proponent of this has been the chief executive of one of the world's largest asset management companies, Blackrock, Larry Fink. He proclaimed in 2018 that: 'companies need to earn their social licence to operate every day'. He added in 2022: 'In today's globally interconnected world, a company must create value for and be valued by its full range of stakeholders in order to deliver long-term value for its shareholders.'[98]

These are not fuzzy ideas—albeit readily dismissed as woke capitalism by some—but genuine attempts to rephrase the notion of social value (commonly referred to as corporate social responsibility (CSR), the forerunner of the term environment, sustainability and governance (ESG)), through responsible investment strategies. The more embedded an organisation is in its stakeholder community, the more resilient it is likely to be as those around can offer support in a crisis.

It is entirely possible for businesses to make a difference while making a profit but with so many truly global challenges then the wider social purpose of organisations should be sought by employers and consumers alike. This can only be through good stewardship which, according to Sir Ian Andrews, a British former senior civil servant (permanent under-secretary of state): 'involves leaders thinking of themselves as transient caretakers, responsible and accountable for the well-being of an organisation which does not belong to them and which they need to pass on in better shape than when they received it rather than simply, and narrowly, as an owner of the shares. It involves thinking in terms of outcomes rather than simply inputs and outputs.'[99]

Out of organisational purpose should emerge a well-defined and articulated set of values. These should be authentic, legitimate and translatable. They should set out the principles and behaviours that are unique to the organisation and by which standards can be set and measured. A set of core values or morals should also drive the individual human spirit and be central to an employee's identity. At a time when people and organisations are feeling anxious, if not lost, by external events then some rephrasing or even restating of a company's values may be helpful.

Roz Brewer points out that 87 per cent of consumers bought products based on values or because a company spoke out on an issue they cared about. This is not always easy as factionalism and partisanship are prevalent characteristics in many of today's societies. Yet, research carried out by consultancy Global Tolerance showed that 42 per cent of employees would rather work for companies that have a positive impact on their communities and strong ethical values.[100]

In fact, ethics mattered more to them than earning a high salary. The difference was even more pronounced among millennials (born between 1981 and 1996) with 64 per cent saying they would not work for a company that did not show strong CSR practices.[101]

Research in consumer behaviour has indicated that it is possible to identify six internal (self-directed or personal) values and three external values (relations-oriented or interpersonal).[102]

These are known as the list of values (LOV) in management studies. The personal values are: self-respect, warm relationships, sense of accomplishment, self-fulfilment, fun and enjoyment, and excitement. The interpersonal ones are: sense of belonging, being well respected, and security. Using a survey model, it is possible to score the identified values which may be helpful to understand the nature of consumers for a target market.

Other models have been proposed based on survey data. In the *theory of basic human values* (2012), Shalom Schwartz arranges ten values in terms of growth versus protection, and personal versus social focus. Each value is distinguished by an underlying motivation or goal.[103]

All of these values can be included in any discussion of individual resilience—they are all relevant to help make a resilient person. Schwartz lists the values as: self-direction, simulation, hedonism, achievement, power, security, conformity, tradition, benevolence, and universalism. He offers a way (the Schwartz Value Survey) of scoring the values identified and generating value priorities. His conclusion is that there is a 'high level of consensus regarding the relative importance of the ten values across societies'. He goes on to draw distinctions between values and attitudes, beliefs, traits or norms which can explain why individuals behave as they do.

Quite understandably, individual companies have developed their own set of values. Mark Zuckerberg announced Meta's new company values in early 2022 in a letter to all company employees. The letter emphasised Meta's vision for the future and the change from Facebook's previous statement of values which was to: 'Give people the power to build community and bring the world closer together.' The new values were to be: move fast; focus on long-term impact; build awesome things; live in the future; be direct and respect your colleagues; Meta, Metamates, Me. Zuckerberg signed off his letter with the words: 'At the end of the day, values aren't what you write on a website but what we hold each other accountable for every day. I encourage you to reflect on these values and what they mean to you as we start working on this next chapter for our company.'[104]

By way of contrast, the oil giant BP has five core values that are said to be crucial to its mission, namely, the safety of its workforce and people, respect, excellence, courage, and one team. This is an interesting mix of ethical and business values. Unilever's values on the other hand are: integrity, respect, responsibility and pioneering into practice. The values of the European Union are: human dignity, freedom, democracy, equality, rule of law, and human rights. At the Mansion House speech in October 2023, King Charles III spoke of the "deep well" of shared values, of "civility and tolerance", the space to "think and speak freely", and the "duty of care" we owe one another. "Rarely have our public wells of civility run so dry," he claimed.[105]

Some common values may become more prominent over time or certainties may be challenged with changing circumstances. The COVID-19 pandemic, for example, has brought the value of health and well-being (particularly mental health) to the top of the priority list for many organisations. Similarly, climate change has placed the ESG agenda high on the priority list, although the issue of 'greenwashing' has caused some global investors to shy away from ethical funding. In fact, Blackrock's Larry Fink has said that he has stopped using ESG criteria because it had become 'weaponised' by politicians from both left and right.[106] Nonetheless, the ESG acronym has been expanded to ESG+R to reflect the importance of resilience in the value agenda.[107]

To the list, and relevant to any rephrased agenda, can be added other values such as stewardship, community and agility. Reflecting the importance of the subject, the European Union has strengthened its supervision of the ESG agenda by introducing the mandatory Corporate Sustainability Reporting Directive (CSRD) for all EU businesses, including qualifying EU subsidiaries of non-EU companies.[108] From 2024 the CSRD aims to help investors, analysts, consumers and other stakeholders better evaluate sustainability performance, resilience and the related business impacts and risks. This directive makes ESG reporting a significant, board-level priority and ensures the philosophy behind ESG remains pertinent.

Looking further afield, the long-running and extensive *World Values Survey* looks at how four sets of values change over time.[109] Traditional values emphasise the importance of religion, parent-child ties, deference to authority and traditional family values. This contrasts with secular-rational values that have the opposite preferences to the traditional ones. Survival values, on the other hand, place an emphasis on economic and physical security. This contrasts with self-expression values which give high priority to environmental protection, growing tolerance of foreigners, gender equality, and rising demands for participation in decision-making in economic and political life.

The common idea that basic values tend to converge as people get richer is only partially true as evidence shows the differences between how people think in different parts of the world seem to be widening. The premise is that as populations become more prosperous, educated, live longer and feel more secure, their descendants become more secular and self-expressive in their moral values. This should make them more resilient. However, the latest findings for 2017–2022 suggest that the speed at which this shift happens varies greatly in different countries.

In some places, it even goes into reverse. Different generations adjust more or less readily, and governments can intervene to slow things down if it suits them. Hence, getting wealthier is not necessarily enough to trigger the shift in values because countries that are getting richer can often feel less secure.

The military represents its set of values through doctrine. In the UK, although each of the four service branches (i.e., navy, army, air force and civil service) defines its own set of values and standards, they have much in common. They are listed as: commitment; loyalty; service; integrity; honesty; objectivity; impartiality; excellence; courage; discipline and respect; and maintaining high standards of compliance with the law, professionalism and personal behaviour.[110]

As doctrine is 'that which is taught', the values and standards are imbued throughout the duration of duty of all service personnel. Without a doubt, war tests this perception to the extreme. When rephrasing private-sector values for greater resilience, it would be worth reflecting on these basics and whether they need to be vocally expressed in some form of corporate doctrine.

The glue that binds together purpose and values is culture. This is even more important than strategy; 'culture eats strategy for breakfast' runs the aphorism.[111] Yet, like the word resilience itself, culture is hard to pin down or document and therefore often overlooked in the search for success. Culture resides in the quotidian exchanges between colleagues and in the hidden threads of routine decisions. It is reflected in the values, beliefs, morals and customs that are codified by an organisation and is increasingly coming under scrutiny by employees and stakeholders alike, including regulators.

Culture has several essential dimensions, namely the tone set from the top (i.e., leadership messages), accountability (i.e., responsibility for managing their risks), effective communication and challenge (both up and down the organisation), and incentives (i.e., alignment with objectives and driving the right behaviours). Ultimately, the leadership and management skills of the executive management in championing these aspects are fundamental to ensuring a strong and healthy culture. They will guide behaviours and expectations on all sides.

Setting behaviours and especially changing them can be a slow process. It takes time, persuasion and encouragement. The journey can be set back more easily than it can be established. Bearing this in mind, it is perhaps surprising how few companies devote time and effort to this aspect of resilience.

In the process of rephrasing, it may be beneficial to re-examine and, if necessary, reformulate a culture statement, sometimes called a culture code, that can be a guide to which employees refer. Such a statement could be composed of various cultural aspects of the company, including the vision, purpose, values, standards, practices, expectations and traditions. Workplace culture statements should be provided to all new employees in the onboarding process, and they should be readily available for employees throughout their tenure. An example of a basic culture statement could be: 'We're building a place of belonging. To create an inspirational company, we believe it is a place where employees can do their best work and be their best selves. We prioritise diversity and believe in a culture rooted in collaboration, growth and mobility.'[112]

Roz Brewer believes that 'culture needs to be at the centre of success' and 'culture and values will be key drivers of motivation for workers as we rephrase the corporate environment'.[113] Post the pandemic, and with organisations facing new working patterns and practices, as well as challenges around the retention of staff, it will be evermore important that employees buy into the corporate purpose, values and culture. To do so is sure to make that organisation more resilient as it will operate as a coherent whole. A start can be made by rephrasing existing approaches.

If culture is the glue that binds together purpose and values, then leadership is the element that sets the parameters for both. Ethical business practices are easier to pursue when one of the core values is leadership, with accountability closely following. Good leadership should display all the stated ethical values of an organisation, setting an example for everyone to follow. They cultivate an environment where people want to adopt the values for themselves.

Leadership is a commitment to excellence through ethical decision-making. If management is about climbing the rungs of a ladder, leadership is about determining the right wall against which the ladder should be placed. [114] Leaders, whether involved in large or small organisations, and particularly in a post-COVID world, need to make decisions when the wall is often less than complete.

The task is made even more difficult when employees are dispersed and may be anxious, when inequalities beyond one's normal authority are heightened, and volatility in the marketplace reigns. Platitudes and policies are no longer sufficient—doing nothing or avoiding harm is no longer good enough either. Yet, leadership plays a crucial role long before and well after a crisis, not just in the epicentre of it. It is a slow-burn issue that needs constant attention and exercise: like trust and reputation, it takes time to develop yet can quickly be undermined by a false step.

Aligned to leadership is the ethical value of stewardship. Stewardship is commonly viewed as the acceptance or assignment of responsibility to shepherd and safeguard an organisation or its employees. It goes beyond the formal leadership management of specific places and people to provide a practical opportunity to create valuable communities for the longer term. The UK Stewardship Code (2020) issued by the Financial Reporting Council, for instance, states that: 'Stewardship is the responsible allocation, management and oversight of capital to create long-term value for clients and beneficiaries leading to sustainable benefits for the economy, the environment and society.'[115]

Sir Ian Andrews believes that: 'Effective stewardship involves taking account of the interests of all stakeholders, both internal and external, and including the wider economy and society which too often unknowingly subsidise that wealth creation. All are vital to the medium- and long-term sustainability of the enterprise; this is equally true in the private, public or not-for-profit sectors.' [116] This is shareholder capitalism over stakeholder capitalism.

Those organisations that have a sound vision, purpose and (strategic) plan are also more likely to have a dedicated workforce that will show the values of loyalty and respect. They are important qualities, particularly in times of shock or stress. According to a survey of 300 business leaders across the US, UK and Europe, 79 per cent of employees, customers and investors say they expect leaders to demonstrate behaviours that drive wider corporate social value (e.g., CSR). 'Societal leadership is now expected to be a core function of business.'[117]

We have come a long way since the early days of those Greco-Roman thinkers on ethical values. At the same time, we have not progressed significantly in realising how to put those values into practice; we continue to struggle to adopt 'moral excellence' as the distractions and deviations have multiplied over the millennia. Despite the time elapsed, we have the same human frailties and inner demons that prevent us from excelling in many respects.

This deficit, placed on a larger plain, has resulted in the disappointing quality of leadership in both the public and private worlds. It has hindered our collective advancement and will also continue to affect our collective resilience. If we are to inspire the young to value what their forefathers struggled for—a better life—then we need to persuade modern society that it can work for them also. Leaders need to focus on delivering long-term prosperity while teachers need to inform and enthuse young people and immigrants that societal values still matter, and they have a stake in generating that prosperity. At the same time, they must show the importance of individual responsibility and social awareness.

An alternative view of how to realise values was offered by the French philosopher, Jean-Jacques Rousseau (d.1778). Rousseau believed that civilisation was not as good a thing as everyone had always assumed: it was not even value-neutral but a bad thing. He believed that human society is a collective being with a will of its own that is different from the sum of the wills of its individual members and that the citizen should be subordinate to this 'general will'.

This introduces the idea of mutual responsibility over self-interest. In fact, Rousseau believed that civilisation is a corrupter of true values, not as people tend to assume their creator and facilitator. He thought that the general will would be better achieved through people coming together rather than voting as in the old Greek city-states, current Swiss cantons or citizen assemblies in general.

Rousseau's philosophy challenges the notion of individual freedom and heralds an authoritarian or anarchist state. He envisaged the power of feeling and instinct over reason, a sentiment that has an attraction, particularly with the young. The ideas had a strong influence on the French Revolution of 1789. When surveyed today, a sizeable proportion of individuals is willing to neglect constitutional or parliamentary checks and balances and would welcome an authoritarian leader rather than a democratic one—a worrying prospect but one that is appearing increasingly in counties around the world.[118]

While authoritarian regimes, including terrorist organisations, have a certain resilient capacity, if only through the application of power and force, their resiliency cannot last as the values they espouse are incoherent and unsustainable over the longer term. In the meanwhile, they can cause untold havoc and misery to millions. It rests on good political leadership, protecting the legitimacy and resilience of our electoral processes of whatever kind, and directing that moral compass and its associated values to as many corners of our civilisation as possible. Sound leadership will also prevent, or at least reduce, a growing and alarming schism in values between the ruling class of people at the top and those working at the bottom, a schism which is giving rise to popular voices demanding a shift in political thinking because of perceived 'values ignored and virtues denied'.[119] The schism may see formerly great and democratic nations come apart at the seams, with potentially violent consequences.

Chapter 6
Seeking Trust and Truth

Whoever is careless with the truth in small matters cannot be trusted with important matters.
— **Albert Einstein**

It is hard to improve on the following introduction to a chapter on trust and truth, concepts which are discrete, but their close affiliation can be measured by the single letter change in the two words. The *Internet Encyclopaedia of Philosophy* states that: 'Trust is a topic of long-standing philosophical interest because it is indispensable to the success of almost every kind of coordinated human activity, from politics and business to sport and scientific research. Even more, trust is necessary for the successful dissemination of knowledge and, by extension, for nearly any form of practical deliberation and planning that requires us to make use of more information than we can gather individually and verify ourselves. In short, without trust we could achieve few of our goals and would know very little.'[120]

In fact, the philosopher Lars Svendsen goes further with his assessment: 'Without trust you would not be able to do anything at all. Imagine a day where you have to calculate all the risks that might come your way, and make sure of the outcome in advance. You would hardly make it out of the front door in the morning. A lack of trust has the obvious consequence that behaviour that presupposes trust will not take place.'[121]

It is therefore unsurprising that trust is an essential component of resilience.[122] If we can trust the people around us, we are more likely to persist with difficult tasks through thick and thin, realising that mutual assurance and confidence are likely to be rewarded with overall success. Generally, we are ready to trust and share with those with whom we have something in common. Trust when combined with shared beliefs and behaviours has been shown to improve recovery rates and instil resilience.[123] It is part of the 'social capital'—described by the sociologist and philosopher Francis Fukuyama—that 'binds people together' in any recovery from major traumas or shocks.[124]

Truth is a separate concept but one that is also part of resilience. Trust and truth are not directly related: trust is not necessarily an affirmation of truth. You can be trusted but not tell the truth: witness the rise of one prominent American politician as an example. If truth is most often used to mean being in accord with the facts or reality, trust is more commonly used in the context of confidence in the integrity and surety of a person. If that person is both true and trusted, s/he is likely to be reliable.

Both parties should feel secure. When mistrust or fear creep in then personal relationships and social order can quickly fracture. Once those enemies gain a presence, it is hard to displace. To adapt an old Dutch saying, 'Trust comes on foot and leaves on horseback.' Trust and truth are both ethereal entities and have value only when exchanged.

It is worth making the early point that trust and trustworthiness are also not the same terms, particularly from a philosophical point of view. The Canadian philosopher Carolyn McLeod believes that: 'Trust is an attitude that we have towards people whom we hope will be trustworthy, where trustworthiness is a property not an attitude.' [125] Another writer poses the question of whether trust can be considered as 'doing' with trustworthiness as 'being'.[126] The focus of this chapter is on trust as a general principle or value, and its relationship to the truth in regard to resilience.

We rely on trust to fulfil many of our daily and lifetime tasks. It is the bedrock of support offered to others and relies on their support in return, often intensified in times of personal crisis or stress. Nonetheless, it requires a leap of faith by at least one of the parties and hence contains an element of risk. This means it can be misplaced (betrayal) but is usually not the starting point in a relationship. Yet, if the situation and motives are strong, trust can release powerful forces. Soldiers will lay down their lives trusting in a greater cause and in others around them. It also relies on good leadership at both the political and military levels. At the same time, it is commonly recognised that: 'Truth is the first casualty of war.'

The English philosopher John Locke (d.1704) believed that legitimate political power rested on trust. It is derived from a sort of contract between members of a society but it cannot itself be a matter of definite contractual rights and duties. Rather, it is exercised by elected politicians in accordance with their own best judgement. People need government and if it is to serve their best interests, they need to be able to trust it.

This proposition leads to the notion of a social contract between politicians and the people. A social contract is typically based on the principle that individuals have consented, either explicitly or tacitly, to surrender some of their freedoms and submit to an authority in exchange for the protection of their remaining rights or maintenance of social order. The term takes its name from *The Social Contract* (1762), a treatise by Jean-Jacques Rousseau that discussed the foundations of a society based on the sovereignty of the 'general will'. Although the antecedents of social contract theory are found in Greek and Stoic philosophy and Roman and Canon Law, the heyday of the social contract was the mid-seventeenth to early nineteenth centuries when it emerged as the leading doctrine of political legitimacy.

John Locke was also a strong proponent of the idea that a government's legitimacy comes from the citizens' delegation to the government of their rights in return for security by the state. This view contrasted with another contemporary English philosopher, Thomas Hobbes (d.1679), who believed that in the absence of a higher authority to adjudicate disputes, everyone feared and mistrusted everyone else, and there could be no justice, commerce or culture. That unsustainable condition came to an end when individuals agreed in a social contract to relinquish their natural rights to everything and to transfer their self-sovereignty to a higher civil authority.

This philosophical debate has resonance today, four centuries after they were articulated, and has relevance for resilience. Locke's view could be ascribed to modern liberal democracies while Hobbes's interpretation could be linked to autocracies with titular heads of government or state. It could be argued that the latter is better placed to implement resilience across a nation from the top down. The state can specify and apply rules and resources as deemed fit for the circumstances and for achieving the desired ends. However, resilience is better applied from the bottom up.

It is individuals and organisations who will have to carry out the essential work to get a country or community back on its feet. This means tackling issues such as inequality, poverty, injustice and ill-health. Good resilience will successfully combine the top-down and bottom-up approaches in harmony. All this depends on trust at both the individual level (friendship) and the political level (verification). It makes trust both conditional and contextual, according to Ben Ansell in the *2023 Reith Lectures*.[127]

As a social contract is often undocumented (without a written constitution), it assumes a high degree of trust between leaders and led. That trust stemming from democratic legitimacy is being stained by the polarisation of attitudes in modern politics. Trust, alongside confidence and compliance, is breaking down and, consequently, the ability of the population to show national or even community resilience is weakening.

The bonds of social cohesion are under severe strain in many liberal democracies. This is documented in an independent UK report—the *Khan Review* (2024)—which has identified social cohesion as an important aspect of a nation's well-being and democratic norms. The report states that social cohesion: 'has wide reaching benefits for society as a whole. From helping achieve sustainable economic growth to reducing the threat of terrorism and hate crime, increasing societal resilience to shocks such as pandemics, improving public health, increasing volunteering and strengthening communities, social cohesion benefits a wide range of adjacent policy areas.' [128] The report wisely advocates a strategic approach to developing social cohesion and believes that without such an approach 'we will witness a slow erosion of the democratic rights and freedoms that are the bedrock of our nation'.

The COVID-19 experience (including post-event inquiries) has accelerated the trend of social dislocation. Without strong leadership and in the absence of a singular 'threat' such as a pandemic then resilience is hard to muster. It cannot be quickly generated in the face of an imminent crisis but requires careful preparation and resourcing. When it does occur, there is no more powerful combination of people and processes to deliver a shared purpose.

Danny Kruger, a British parliamentarian, has proposed a 'social covenant' because he believes it is both more substantial and less transactional than a social contract.[129] He believes the new social model we need should be more trusting, more entrepreneurial, and provide an opportunity to level up across the country, but this would require a greater transfer of power and wealth to our communities. Kruger writes: 'The "deal" implied in the social covenant is one of mutual responsibility—there is work for individual citizens, for civil society (including businesses) and for the state (meaning public services, central and local government).' The four 'articles' which he suggests the government should adopt as a set of principles are: public purpose, subsidiarity and inclusion, strength-based approaches, and social infrastructure.

In return, social or shared responsibility from individuals, communities and organisations must be forthcoming. The idea of public service as a responsibility of citizens needs to be revitalised but will not happen without trust in the ruling party and a clear route to how it is to be achieved. The notion of a whole-of-society approach to resilience has been articulated in a national resilience framework by the UK government: this is not a strategy along the lines of other priority government policies. The framework is a worthy idea but as yet no clear mechanism has been put forward to achieve across-the-board resilience; in other words, resilience in the round. Other countries have made more progress under whole-of-nation or total-defence labels.

To emphasise the shortfall in strategic thinking, a report by the UK's National Audit Office in 2023 stated that: 'The UK Resilience Framework does not set out a well-defined vision for what a resilient UK looks like, including targets and standards for the desired level of national, local or sectoral resilience.' 'Without these, government cannot make informed decisions about trade-offs between long- and short-term priorities, investment or funding allocation of priority areas. It also makes it difficult for government or other stakeholders to track progress and evaluate how effectively and efficiently government is using public funds to improve national resilience.'[130] Unless and until these deficits are addressed head-on, it is unlikely that resilience will mature to its highest potential in UK politics.

Thinkers and writers have suggested a variety of attributes that can be linked to trust. A former US special forces officer, Rich Diviney, believes there are four attributes to trust: competency (i.e., I trust you to do the thing right), consistency (i.e., I trust you to do the thing right over time), integrity (i.e., I trust you to do the right thing), and compassion (i.e., I trust you to do the right thing for someone because you care about them as a human being).[131]

Diviney offers techniques to put these attributes into practice. There are many other suggestions but most have common components in play. Examples include honesty, reliability, goodwill and accountability. The Harvard Business School, for instance, offers three elements: positive relationships, good judgement/expertise, and consistency.[132] In its research work and surveys, it found that while 'inconsistency does have a negative impact (trust went down by 17 points), it was relationships that had the most substantial impact. When relationships were low and both judgment and consistency were high, trust went down by 33 points.'

Two components seem to be missing from these lists that describe the key ingredients of trust and are integral to resilience; they may be there in some part by inference or default. One is communication, the other is leadership. A major component of trust is being able to communicate with your fellows with transparency. That can be achieved, to some degree, via digital (social) media or distant phone calls but to be truly effective it needs personal, face-to-face contact.

You need to see and speak to the person in order to build a rapport and gain a mutual appreciation which can build the necessary bonds. Good communication helps establish those positive relationships mentioned by Harvard Business School. Social media, while promising to build communities, cannot achieve this aspect alone. Rather, it allows relationships to exist in the ether without experiencing the hard interfaces, the reality of human interactions.

Leadership is the other factor in delivering trust and by association resilience. This is true at all levels of both public- and private-sector organisations. A survey by a business advisory company underscores the growing engagement of senior management, including the C-suite, with one in five respondents emphasising that the ultimate responsibility for resilience rests with them.[133]

Although not surveyed, the same degree of responsibility should fall on governments and politicians. Leaders, whether political, corporate or not-for-profit, need to show that they can rise to the multiple and concurrent challenges by providing a hopeful vision that unites and pervades. It means acting positively and being counted in the pursuit of values and principles. Above all, leaders need to display and promote resilience to the risks materialising. In fact, risk is determined less by a realistic appraisal of the threat and more by the nature and style of leadership. Effective leadership at the top should remove the all-too-frequent disconnect between strategic risk and operational resilience.

Another annual and large survey, the *2023 Edelman Trust Barometer*, makes some gloomy assertions.[134] It states that: 'A lack of faith in societal institutions triggered by economic anxiety, disinformation, mass-class divide and a failure of leadership has brought us to where we are today—deeply and dangerously polarised.' Survey results show that distrust breeds polarisation. The conclusion is that business is the only institution seen as competent and ethical, and CEOs are 'obligated to improve economic optimism and hold divisive forces accountable'. There is what is described as a 'battle for truth', with 'A shared media environment [that] has given way to echo chambers, making it harder to collaboratively solve problems. Media is not trusted, with especially low trust in social media.'

The *Edelman Barometer* claims that government and the media fuel a cycle of distrust, and are seen as sources of misleading information. One of the ways forward that is proposed is to advocate for the truth i.e., for it to be a source of reliable information, promote civil discourse and hold information sources accountable. The concerns of societal polarisation are also echoed in the *World Economic Forum Global Risk Report 2024*. That document states that: 'As polarisation grows and technological risks remain unchecked, "truth" will come under pressure.' [135] Misinformation (falsehoods) and disinformation (deliberately misleading) are recorded as the most severe global risks anticipated over the next two years. They are some of the key challenges to resilience, increasing the likelihood of bad outcomes as well as impeding response and recovery capabilities.

Certain industries are more trusted than others. Farmers are the most trusted by European consumers overall—about two-thirds (67 per cent) of those asked in 2020 indicate trust in them, compared to just 13 per cent that do not. Retailers are the next most trusted with around a half (53 per cent) trusting against a fifth who do not.[136] When asked who was least trusted, the top sectors identified by consumers were automotive/garages, tech/social media, insurance and government. This provides opportunities for brands in these sectors—if they can increase engagement and build trust—to differentiate themselves from rivals and increase overall revenues.

We are certainly in a post-truth period which has 'developed from a shorthand label for the abundance and influence of misleading or false political claims'.[137] Truth, though powerless, possesses its own strength and allows challenges to whatever alternative facts those in power may contrive. While persuasion and violence can destroy truth, they cannot replace it. This is true for secular or religious truth as much as factual truth.[138]

We feel we live in an age of conspiracy theories, fake news (elevated by the misuse of artificial intelligence), propaganda, disinformation and misinformation. Yet, those negative qualities have been around for millennia. The early scholars, theologians and philosophers wrestled with the concept of truth proposing various theories around truth (metaphysics), but they and their successors have faced the same dilemmas of unwrapping what is true and false outside of perhaps mathematics. Modern social media has certainly allowed these attributes to flourish as people rely on the information packaged in short bursts coming across their illuminated screens rather than traditional media outlets.

For those trying to recover from trauma then truth is crucial if one is to have faith in what information is being offered (and/or the person offering it), even if that information is not complete at the time. Reliance on the facts as presented offers a foothold from which to step up to a higher plane of recovery with confidence and clarity. If alternative facts are presented through propaganda, conspiracies or plain lies then the foothold is weakened and will likely lead to erroneous coping mechanisms. This does not mean that the untruths are not persuasive or compelling. In fact, depending on the potency of the storyteller and the susceptibility of the recipient, they may tempt belief in the alternative.

The English philosopher and Franciscan friar William of Ockham (d.1347) offered some wise words when dealing with facts. His principle, commonly known as Ockham's Razor, states that of two alternative explanations of the same phenomena then the more complicated is more likely to have something wrong with it. Therefore, with other things being equal, the simpler is the more likely to be correct. If this is true, we should assume, in the course of trying to work out an explanation of something, the minimum. At first sight, this may be counterintuitive as we tend to give weight to complexity but if simplicity can help reveal the truth and thereby gain trust then it is worth pursuing.

Researchers of facts, alternative facts and fact-checking in post-truth politics have made some interesting observations. In a randomised online experiment during the 2017 French Presidential election campaign, they subjected subgroups of 2,480 French voters to alternative facts by the extreme-right candidate, Marine Le Pen, and/or corresponding facts about the European refugee crisis from official sources. They found that: first, alternative facts are highly persuasive; second, fact-checking improves the factual knowledge of voters; third, fact-checking does not affect policy conclusions or support for the candidate; and, fourth, exposure to facts alone does not decrease support for the candidate, even though voters update their knowledge.[139]

This mixed message offers both hope and concern. If knowing the truth does not sway listeners, there remains a lot to do in educating people on the dangers of actions based on 'alternative facts'. This should also involve advice and training on how best to sift the wheat from the chaff, and techniques to verify what is being proposed. As President Ronald Regan once said, it is important to trust but verify.

Another way of improving the situation in organisations is to give people greater influence over their ability to assess the facts and hence determine the truth for themselves. Empowerment is the process whereby responsibility—but not authority—is devolved downwards to employees who can then act on their own experience and judgement to resolve issues. Through this mechanism, it is incumbent on people to ascertain the facts before acting, hence reinforcing the true state of affairs.

To be effective, empowerment needs to be based on a high level of trust which comes about through good situational awareness and team bonding as well as mutual confidence, all built up over time. Empowerment without context and mutuality can lead to chaos. In the book *Humanocracy* (2020), the authors believe that routine, low-skilled jobs can be improved when employees in those jobs are given the opportunity to use their initiative and change the way they work.[140]

The authors report: 'What makes a job low-skilled is not the nature of the work it entails, or the credentials required, but whether or not the people performing the task have the opportunity to grow their capabilities and tackle novel problems.' They can do this while discovering the facts to help problem-solving. This makes trust and truth essential ingredients for not only engaging people in meaningful occupations but also ensuring that they can contribute to a stronger, more reflective society.

Chapter 7
Coping with Change

If you change the way you look at things, the things you look at change.
— Wayne Dyer

Change has become a prominent feature of our complex world and to cope with it we need to be increasingly agile and adaptive. These characteristics, alongside the whole change process, are central to the concept of resilience. As resilience is more about bouncing forward to a new state than bouncing back to the old one, change must be integral. In order to build a better system out of the disruption, it is necessary to be dynamic, flexible and responsive in the face of potential opposition, intransigence and insecurity. Such ideas have been a central tenet of the philosophy of resilience for millennia.

One of the earliest issues was the dialogue around permanence and change. Beginning with the first known philosopher, Thales of Miletus (d.c548 BC), Greek thinkers were challenged by the occurrence of natural change alongside the continuance of apparently permanent conditions. The earliest theories attempted to account for this by portraying the world in terms of certain constant elements which constitute the 'real' or permanent aspect, while the rest was in flux in the world of 'appearance'. The latter might continually alter but the former always retained the same basic aspects. However, it was acknowledged that the two aspects could on occasion be incompatible.

Another early Greek philosopher, Heraclitus of Ephesus (d.c500 BC), believed that everything in the universe was a river of flux. He used an allegorical story of a river to explain that, like a river, nature flowed ever onwards and was constantly changing. He believed that you could not step into the same river twice. This was because the river was constantly changing. When we stepped into the river, withdrew, and when we stepped in for a second time, we encountered different water and thus a different river. Our experience had changed and the first instance could not be repeated or recaptured. We stepped into and out of the river as different beings.

Aristotle accepted that objects change. He offered a solution that combined the two states of permanence and change by saying that something which remains the same can also be subject to variation: an oak tree has leaves in the summer but not in the winter, for instance. Aristotle believed that we should accept that the natural world is made up of a series of processes that are constantly changing if we want to live in harmony with it.

A refusal to embrace change as a necessary and normal part of life can readily lead to problems and disappointment. On the other hand, acceptance (albeit not resignation) that everything is constantly changing and fleeting may allow life to run more smoothly. Change can be liberating and opens prospects which would not occur but for change. To ignore or contest change may be remiss and regressive.

The Stoics and subsequent thinkers acknowledged that all this is easier said than done. The natural tendency is often to resist change as it potentially threatens stability, safety, security and sometimes relationships and may foretell adversity. Many writers and philosophers have grappled with our impulse to resist it. 'Something in us wishes to remain a child…to reject everything strange,' wrote the Swiss psychiatrist Carl Jung (d.1961), echoing Heraclitus.[141]

The natural resistance to change can limit learning and innovation, and deny the realisation of new opportunities. Yet, these are future potentials which often do not counterbalance more immediate and prevailing concerns and protections. As remarked in *Chapter 2*, Stoicism as a philosophy is not so much about resisting change as facing up to it and appreciating the present while accepting that it is not forever.

Thinkers have developed different theories and ideas on the process of change up to the present day. Julia Samuel, a modern British psychotherapist, believes that accepting change also makes one better at it. She writes: 'It's the paradox that the more you allow yourself to accept that change is inevitable, the more likely you are to change intentionally and adapt.'[142]

Change can be an engine of progress, the 'proof of vigour'. In fact, the only lasting truth is change itself, and we need to reconcile ourselves to cope with it. As the *Serenity Prayer* advocates: 'God, grant me the serenity to accept the things I cannot change, the courage to change the things I can, and the wisdom to know the difference.' [143]

One philosopher who is worthy of note in this brief introduction to change is Georg Hegel (d.1831) because he provided the foundation for Marxism. Hegel introduced a law or rationality of change which postulated that understanding reality involves understanding the process of change. Hegel believed that change is a dialectical process that begins with an action (thesis) that generates a reaction (antithesis) which resolves itself in a new situation (synthesis). Because synthesis contains the potential for fresh conflicts, so begins a new cycle of change. This, says Hegel, is why nothing ever stays the same. Heraclitus and Aristotle et al would surely agree.

The contemporary Austrian philosopher Karl Popper (d.1994) mounted a counterargument to the ideas of Plato and Marx by saying that the creation and perpetuation of an ideal society are out of reach in our complex world.

What is important is to manage the process of endless change and engage in perpetual problem-solving. Popper believed we should concentrate on seeking out the worst social ills and removing them. This translates into spending less time on building model schools and hospitals and more on getting rid of the worst ones, hence improving the lot of people. Popper's ideas have presented one of the most compelling cases for democratic openness and tolerance in modern times.

To be able to drive forward the notion of problem-solving, agility and adaptation come to the fore. It is now time to examine these two attributes in more detail, having gained the insights of some notable philosophical minds. The terms have a close affiliation—perhaps two sides of the same coin—but can occur separately as well as in partnership. Both are required for resilience to take hold. By themselves, however, they will not necessarily deliver resilience. If resilience is the goal, agility and adaptation are techniques to facilitate the journey.

Agility—from the ancient Greek *ágō*, meaning to lead or guide—is the age-old concept of reacting quickly and easily, to be fleet of foot in the face of dynamic circumstances. In his philosophical treatise, *Summa Theologiae*, Saint Thomas Aquinas explained that: 'slowness of movement would seem especially inconsistent with the nature of a spirit. But the glorified bodies will be most spiritual [...]. Therefore, they will be agile.'[144]

Over the ages, the spirit of agility as applied to people has taken on a different meaning to the one applied to the inner capacity of organisations and networks. In the latter case, being agile is also about not being caught off guard, of being flexible and opportunistic in pursuit of the spirit of the organisation. Today, agility has become a management philosophy in its own right.[145]

Agility requires balance, speed, strength and coordination; above all, it demands a change in thinking or mindset. It is a response to complexity, confusion or challenge that counters paralysis or precipitate action (the 'flight-or-fight' syndrome) and allows new perspectives to arise above the surface noise. Focusing on agility, in combination with resilience, can prepare people to handle uncertainty more successfully by adapting to change more quickly and managing stress more effectively.[146]

It is the synthesis that Hegel talked about. It can also be witnessed in nature as those animals that are agile are more likely to forage successfully, exploit niches over competitors and so evolve as species.

It is commonly assumed that agility is correlated to age: the younger ones of us may be nimbler in the physical and mental senses than those with more years than they care to attribute—just look at the speed with which youngsters deal with modern technology and new challenges. However, experience and expertise, especially in a crisis, count favourably as agility has a component that requires a careful evaluation of the challenges to avoid nugatory work in finding solutions. That experience is also valuable in team building and empowerment. Whatever the age of an individual, an entrepreneurial and innovative drive can be encouraged to reinforce agility.

Agility can best be witnessed in organisations that have created new teams or groups or repurposed existing ones to act as rapid decision-making bodies in the event of a crisis or disruption. These new bodies often begin life as crisis-management teams composed of the most senior people who meet regularly to make decisions and reallocate resources quickly. The reinvigorated structures can allow organisations to cut the usual red tape and management layers that slow decision-making. Decisions that previously required hard-won consensus or an onerous burden of proof could be accelerated if they can be overtly aligned to the organisation's common purpose.[147]

Agility can readily be facilitated by technology. Yet, an agile organisation thinks of technology not as a supporting capability but as a core element that is seamlessly integrated into every aspect of that organisation.[148] Modern computing, including cloud computing, mobile telephony, and generative artificial intelligence, has allowed—and will increasingly do so—response times to escalate exponentially. We can now interact with others at anytime from anywhere in the world via a spider's web of interconnectivity. While beneficial in many respects, particularly conferring network agility, it has inevitable downsides. In terms of mindsets, the reactivity puts a strain on people to match the pace of events and can affect mental health.

Technological developments are also outpacing the human and societal capacity to manage them, as is revealed by the concern of some researchers on future models of artificial intelligence. This notwithstanding, there is now such a dependency on technology working effectively all the time that when it does not work, we crash like the machines themselves. Previous workaround skills are not just redundant but forgotten: pen and paper are old school.

The idea of having a reserve or spare capacity—the principle of redundancy—has grown in organisations in recent times. Such redundancy confers agility as one can deal with the unexpected with standby capabilities. It is an opportunity to develop slack, whether that be measured in spare resources, reserve stocks, unused capacity or simply time to think.

A network has inbuilt redundancy through the duplication of assets: if one node is lost, another can take its place. This principle gives the internet its strength, for instance. The idea has given rise to the notion of having spare capacity 'just in case' something goes awry rather than the traditionally lean approach of minimising redundancy to meet 'just-in-time' criteria, even accepting that there may be increased costs and reduced efficiency with the former.

Agile organisations typically maintain stable, top-level structures but replace much of the traditional management hierarchy with a flexible, scalable network of teams. They go beyond creating local teams to creating dense networks of groups and systems. They implement clear, flat structures and ensure there is clarity of purpose. Here, the team is at the heart of the structure, and team-based working is a central tenet of agile thinking. It has advantages over a hierarchical structure in terms of speed, precision, decision-making and satisfaction for employees. Today's business depends on its ability to react quickly and adapt to a competitive environment.

Philosophers have had much to say about the topic. Pragmatic philosophy, associated with American thinkers such as William James (d.1910) and John Dewey (d.1952), has focused on the practical consequences of decision-making and the idea that beliefs and actions should be judged by their effectiveness. From a pragmatic perspective, agility (coupled with adaptation) is essential for addressing real-world challenges.

Pragmatists value flexibility and the ability to adjust strategies based on the outcomes they produce. Other philosophers have promoted systems thinking in the debate. Systems thinkers, such as the Austrian biologist Ludwig von Bertalanffy (d.1972), known as the information philosopher, and Gregory Bateson (d.1980), an English anthropologist, have considered the interconnectedness of elements in a system. From this perspective, agility with adaptation is crucial for navigating complex systems. The ability to recognise and respond to feedback loops and changes in the environment is essential for maintaining balance and harmony within a system.

Diversity, both visible (e.g., gender, age, ethnicity) and invisible (e.g., sexual orientation, socio-economic background), can also bring agility to a workforce. In terms of broader resilience, diversity—coupled with inclusion and equality—is essential for providing the widest possible range of options and ideas to allow adaptation to occur across organisations. A diverse system possesses or can draw upon a range of capabilities, information sources and technical elements. The official report on the nuclear accident at Fukushima in 2011 argues that one of the causes of the disaster was a distressing lack of diversity of views.[149]

When it comes to adaptive capacity in nature, the English naturalist Charles Darwin (d.1882) made the point that natural selection was not about the survival of the fittest or about the most intelligent but about those creatures which could adapt the fastest to change. He believed that species evolve and adapt to changing environments, and this idea could be extended to other domains. Yet the concept of adaptation was contemplated long before Darwin. The ancient Greek philosophers such as Empedocles (d.443 BC) and Aristotle made early inroads into our thinking. The former did not believe that adaptation required a cause but thought that it 'came about naturally, since such things survived'. Aristotle did believe in final causes but assumed that species were fixed.[150]

He devoted much time to studying natural history and constructed a 'theory of forms' to explain his biological concepts. In the natural philosophy of the eighteenth and nineteenth centuries, adaptation was taken as evidence for the existence of a deity. In the twenty-first century, adaptation (alongside mitigation) has taken on a powerful note in climate change and the consequences for the human and natural world.

Besides the evolutionary process whereby an organism becomes better able to live in its habitat, adaptation has become a more general aspect of human existence under the banner of resilience. If resilience is the ability to anticipate and absorb shocks and stresses then the key third component—often missing from discussion—is adaptation. Adaptation involves issues such as insight, reorganisation, transformation and learning.

To be adaptive, it is necessary to accept the power of change that can bring opportunities as well as challenges. Adaptation can allow people and groups to find new and imaginative ways of working more collaboratively, making them more efficient and competitive. It can remove barriers, silos and bureaucracy wherever possible so that nimble cross-working becomes the norm. It also encourages empowerment and entrepreneurialism and embraces innovation and technologies that can accelerate processes and decision-making.

Despite the potential benefits, there is often an inherent reluctance to step on the path of adaptation. Traditional structures and operating methods are embedded, codified and defended. As a result, structures that are no longer fit for purpose when the circumstances change are perpetuated well beyond their usefulness. This can be true for geopolitical entities, national or local bodies as well as commercial organisations. Institutional reform can, however, come about because of crises.

The Ukrainian and Palestinian conflicts may well bring about a reconstitution of the military (e.g., NATO) and political (e.g., UN Security Council) structures respectively, ones that have atrophied since they were established. The current period of poly-crisis has highlighted the mismatch between the traditional institutions and the outcomes or quality of effort that those outcomes require. If reconstitution proves too challenging as well as it might, bilateral mediation with efforts at de-escalation and containment is the second-best option.

This would aim to achieve short-term, limited goals such as an agreement that allowed Ukrainian grain to pass through the Black Sea in 2022. Resilience can only endure if efforts to resolve conflicts can allow the parties to build back better. This needs better global governance, or at least whole-of-government approaches across the board, as well as better leadership to ensure an improved quality of effort is injected. Such impetus is currently in short supply, or at least we are swimming against the tide.

Large organisations with complex bureaucracies like multinationals and governments generally have little experience of being, or the capacity to be, adaptive. They are often like a supertanker requiring many sea miles to change direction. It is at the other end of the spectrum—small and medium-sized enterprises—where individuals, teams and groups, especially first responders to an emergency, tend to show the greatest degree of adaptability to changing circumstances. Regrettably, they often lack the resources or power to transfer their adaptive behaviours to larger swathes of society. Both people and groups learn to adapt better when they are organised to be agile.

It is important to note also that adaptation and change are not necessarily easy processes. Changing attitudes and behaviours can take time and may conflict with agility and flexibility. Take, for example, the 'Clunk Click Every Trip' campaign for wearing seat belts to improve road safety in the UK. This began in the early 1970s but actions did not become law until 1983 and only after extensive promotion and societal debate.[151]

The COVID-19 pandemic has also revealed the lengthy efforts to persuade people to wear masks or get vaccinated. Besides the persistent doubters, there is a need for a strong public message to persuade people of the right cause of action. Communicating the appropriate and consistent message is important to change minds.

Whereas adaptation can be achieved through incremental adjustments, transformation involves dramatic change to a new and better state. COVID-19 vaccines enabled governments to transform their response to the pandemic, fundamentally changing the risk-reward calculus for lockdowns and allowing countries to open their economies. Clean energy will prove even more transformative in the future.[152] As challenges mount in geopolitics and business, transformation involving fundamental change will become even more prevalent in our approach to achieving long-term resilience. It will require radical, systemic shifts in values and beliefs, as well as patterns of social behaviour. This will demand high levels of leadership and governance at all levels.

Transformation in people and organisations, as a change technique, can be compared to the process of metamorphosis (from the Greek *meta* meaning after and *morphe* meaning form) in certain animals. This is a biological process by which an animal changes physically and radically from one form, such as a caterpillar, into another, such as a chrysalis, and then into a third form, such as a butterfly. The transformation is often brought about or induced when animals need to change their structure to adapt to new habitats so that they can perpetuate their life cycles.

During metamorphosis in insects, for instance, all the tissues of the insect are completely dissolved to create an internal soup with only highly organised groups of cells known as imaginal discs surviving. (See *Nature's Resilience* (2025)).

The discs use the protein-rich soup in which they sit to fuel the rapid cell division required to form the new wings, antennae, legs, eyes and other features of the adult butterfly. There cannot be anything more transformational, but it is resisted initially by the caterpillar's immune system until the discs win out. One observer has remarked: 'It's the caterpillar's job to resist the butterfly and the butterfly's job to become stronger because of the opposition to its advance.' [153] This tension between change and stasis is commonly reflected in other transformations, human as well as animal.

Aristotle had much to say about transformation. In a valuable exposé of Aristotle's thinking, Pia Lauritzen, a modern Danish philosopher, explains that the ancient thinker made a distinction between expertise, science, wisdom and prudence. [154] Lauritzen sets out those four domains of knowledge in quadrants using two axes: theory and practice on one, and past and present on the other.

She believes the distinction between the domains can provide a framework for understanding what she calls 'the messy middle of transformation', that is where the axes intersect. This is the unknown, uncertain space between past and future, between theory and practice, that characterises organisations in the process of becoming something new. 'To navigate the messy middle of a transformation, leaders must understand how the different knowledge domains contribute to the transformation—and help their employees find a way to be part of the same conversation.'

Pia Lauritzen believes that: 'you must engage and motivate those who are going to carry out the transformation by starting with expertise in the bottom left quadrant (i.e., past and practice) and moving forward by drawing on knowledge from the other three quadrants to achieve transformation.' This constitutes a messy middle ground. She concludes by saying that transformations often fail because 'leaders don't acknowledge the importance of inviting people with different ways of thinking and talking about transformation to join a common conversation. None of the four knowledge domains can exist without the others, and leaders depend on all of them to navigate the messy middle of transformation.' The conclusion emphasises the point about the importance of learning. It was Aristotle who expressed his belief that: 'All learning comes about from already existing knowledge.'

Humans, organisations or infrastructures in the built environment all use transformation to achieve new goals or meet new circumstances when there is sufficient momentum to be radical. According to one consultancy, business transformation is about new ways of working, new capabilities and new technologies.[155] This simple statement conceals a great deal of inner turmoil and tussle. As preserving stability no longer meets the requirements of the time, components become reordered and rebuilt in a revolutionary rather than evolutionary sense.

Yet, it is acknowledged that such 'transformations are not easy to get right'. It is 'difficult, with less than a third of transformations reaching their goals to improve organisational performance and sustain these improvements over time'. Transformation and sustainability go hand in hand. Whether revolutionary transformation or evolutionary change, the Italian Niccolo Machiavelli (d.1527) reminds us in his famous political treatise, *The Prince*, published five years after his death, that: 'There is nothing more difficult to take in hand, more perilous to conduct, or more uncertain in its success, then to take the lead in the introduction of a new order of things. Because the innovator has for enemies all those who have done well under the old conditions, and lukewarm defenders in those who may do well under the new.'[156]

Chapter 8
From Mindset to Skillset

Give the pupils something to do, not something to learn; and the doing is of such a nature as to demand thinking; learning naturally results.

– **John Dewey**

In her book, Carol Dweck writes that it is not intelligence, talent or education that sets successful people apart but rather their mindset and the way that they approach life's challenges. She believes that there are two main mindsets by which we can navigate life; they are growth and fixed.[157] People with a growth mindset view intelligence, abilities and talents as learnable and capable of improvement through their own effort. Conversely, people with a fixed mindset see those same traits as inherently stable and unchangeable over time.

Because of the plasticity of the human brain to form new connections, particularly when stimulated by new experiences, a growth mindset can be adopted at any time of life. Dweck offers steps to achieve this and the technique has become popular in management circles. The Harvard Business School, for instance, has promoted the approach and believes that there are four ways a growth mindset can help advance an organisation: it encourages creativity, it fosters resilience, it facilitates innovation, and it promotes learning.[158]

The fixed versus growth mindset may be a binary approach, ignoring many who use both approaches at different times. Growth is not a universal desire as contentment is also high on the human agenda. Managers should accordingly be aware of individual desires and needs when motivating those under their supervision.

In the context of resilience, there are other ways to view the output of the bilateral human brain. This relates to skill sets which can also be placed in two camps. The first one connects to the left hemisphere of the brain which generally performs tasks that deal with logic and mechanics in human behaviour and activity. These attributes relate to those so-called 'hard skills' that deal with the directional, institutional and technical skills that can be associated with resilience such as planning, policies and practices. They are concrete, measurable abilities that can demonstrate proficiency through certifications, portfolios, assessments, etc. Hence, hard skills are usually obtained through experience or education.

The right hemisphere of the brain on the other hand performs those tasks that deal more with creativity, imagination and artistic representation. In the same vein, the so-called 'soft skills' in resilience deal with the adaptable and personable aspects of resilience such as learning, agility, leadership and trust. Soft skills are typically learnt through education or training and are necessary for most walks of life. They are more akin to personality traits that are developed throughout life and hence are commonly known as durable skills.[159]

This physiological and psychological division is not a rigid delineation, if only because the two sides of the brain are linked and operate as one. As with the growth versus fixed mindset distinction, there is no black and white here but a blend of characteristics that apply to different situations. The hard-soft dichotomy is, however, one that can help in trying to understand that resilience is not a single-faceted attribute, rather it is one that has multiple and diverse aspects. It is best to think of the soft skills complementing the hard ones in a successful realisation of resilience. Both are required to varying degrees.

This notwithstanding, the balance between the soft and hard skill sets has traditionally been inharmonious. The hard skills have generally predominated as they are easier to apply and more tangible to document. A resilience plan, policy, protocol or standard is something that can be recorded and retrieved. Such documents usually form the basis of managerial actions in a crisis and direct recovery operations when activated. Yet, it is the soft skills which are more difficult to apply as they are more behavioural and not readily transferrable to paper or e-file.

They outline the type of culture within which an organisation operates, the degree of empowerment given to employees, the level of trust between leaders and led, and the extent to which learning is encouraged at all levels. Any one of these characteristics can be more influential in determining the success, as well as the reputation, of a company in the face of disruption than any hard skill. However, we seem to be poor at developing the soft skills to anywhere near the same level as the hard ones simply because the former is collectively difficult to inculcate. Until we do, our resilience capacity will suffer as we will not have the full panoply of abilities to draw upon.

To understand further the growth versus fixed or hard versus soft mindsets in our philosophical journey of resilience, it is necessary to examine in more detail four key skills that have a profound impact on the subject. They are: knowledge (and learning), communication (and language), perception (and awareness) and social (and people) skills. These can be considered meta-skills which are transferable abilities and behaviours that help people adapt and succeed in life, study and work. Each has been considered by philosophers down the ages. They will be considered in turn but should be consumed in entirety.

We begin with knowledge and a brief review of philosophical thought. Socrates believed that 'virtue is knowledge' and he pursued knowledge through discussion and argument. He thought that in knowledge lay happiness, and spent his life—as we all do—looking for it. Plato went on to develop a classical 'theory of knowledge' (epistemology) which stated that knowledge was attainable, but it must be both infallible and genuinely real rather than in appearance only. Saint Thomas Aquinas, basing himself on Aristotle, argued that all rational knowledge is acquired through sensory experience, on which our minds reflect. John Locke believed that 'No man's knowledge can go beyond his experience.'

The sixteenth-century French philosopher René Descartes (d.1650) changed the philosophical question from 'how ought we to live?' to 'what can I know?'. 'I think, therefore I am', is the first principle of Descartes's philosophy. With this shift, he put epistemology at the centre of philosophy for the next three centuries. Descartes believed that certainty was available in our knowledge of the world which is acquired through reason.

Sensory input was inherently unreliable and more a source of error than of knowledge. Later philosophers like Karl Popper believed that science produced theories but these were not incorrigible truths and better theories would replace them over time. However, investigations into the nature of knowledge have been science-led for much of the history of Western philosophy.

The philosopher John Dewey believed the problem-solving approach to knowledge—what he called 'learning by doing'—was the best approach as it combined being practical with taking into account the importance of theory. The combination encouraged people to be imaginative and, above all, would train them in general competence in all fields of human activity. His ideas became and remain influential in education worldwide.

Dewey was one of several American philosophers who believed that a statement is true if it accurately describes a situation, prompts us to anticipate experiences correctly, and fits in with other related statements. The concept of pragmatism stresses the priority of action over doctrine and of experience over fixed principles. This accords with the broad notions of resilience.

In general, the philosophical movement has been divided on its view of knowledge into what can be known independently of experience (*a priori*) and what is derived from experience (*a posteriori*). The followers of the former such as Immanuel Kant are generally classified as rationalists while the latter such as John Locke are classified as empiricists. Whatever the source or outcome of knowledge, the dynamic process of acquiring it is classified as learning by way of study, education and training.

Learning *a priori* can begin with directed lessons in school, for instance, but continue with *a posteriori* experiences as indirect lessons learnt: 'one is never too old to learn', as the saying goes. Yet, transferring 'tacit knowledge' from experienced people to those early learners cannot be easily documented or disseminated but is a key and valuable element of organisational development. Success is possible through storytelling and video recordings as part of team building, but this must be done progressively and before the normal churn or retirement of people denies the history pool.

To help people cope with their quotidian challenges and life's changes, and thereby become more resilient, it is also necessary to begin education and training early and widely. Such preparation should cover not only major responses and emergencies but also routine trials and tribulations. People can relate more easily to the latter but may gain more benefits from the former when their lives may be at risk.

Resilience education could help with topics that we rarely discuss, largely because they are painful such as bereavement, unemployment, ill-health, divorce, etc. There is currently limited opportunity to offer coping or problem-solving strategies in these difficult areas. For parents, the hope is that children become more resilient as they develop, almost by an unconscious process of osmosis by absorbing real-life experiences. Schooling can play a part but is limited in all that must be taught. As the educationalist Sir Anthony Seldon has said: 'schools should develop character traits such as resilience, strength to withstand adversity, communication, empathy, and confidence, either intentionally or as part of the "hidden curriculum".'[160]

If a structured and systematic approach could be introduced at scale at work, it would do much for employers and the wider economy. Many employers in a survey believed that we could better prepare children for the world of work through basic workplace skills, including ways to be more resilient.[161] According to the Commercial Education Trust, the UK economy could be boosted by as much as £125 billion if greater focus were given to commercial skills such as resilience, self-motivation and time-keeping within the educational system.[162]

A possible learning programme around resilience should be designed to help young people apply better coping skills to their lives and others around them whatever the circumstances and challenges. It would not remove all forms of anxiety or stress: some inherent tension is an important part of motivation and resilience itself. The programme should be progressive and begin at secondary school and continue at colleges, universities and clubs. Knowledge gained in tertiary education is a great resilience driver. Research by the UK's Office for Students found that graduates tend to be more resilient to life's stresses than non-graduates.[163]

Any programme should not be prescriptive but rather progressive, offering some pointers for continuous improvement. The topics should be around awareness (both self- and situational), self-reliance, perseverance, flexibility, health and well-being, trustworthiness and resourcefulness. These should include real-life examples at the appropriate educational levels and practical tasks, including team building and community-focused projects. They could incorporate some physical or outward-bound training to help strengthen mental resolve and physical robustness.

In employment, resilience education should continue through an established approach to learning lessons and applying new skills. Reskilling or upskilling for new job opportunities as old skills become redundant will make career paths more of a portfolio of experience than it is already. It is likely that people will have a dozen or more career changes throughout their working life as the pace of change picks up. This will mean that people will have to be resilient in the job market and be agile in their search for employment and progression. Diversity of skills and a breadth of knowledge—a multidisciplinary approach—will help people's capabilities remain broad-based and flexible in the face of change. It counters the danger of specialisation as perceptions narrow.

Any consideration of skills brings in the important issue of learning. According to the Socratic Paradox, if we do not know something we would be unable to recognise this knowledge when we learn it: if I can tell the right answer from the wrong one, Socrates argued, I must have already known the right answer. Søren Kierkegaard explained this paradox by saying that instead of explaining knowledge as a recollection, it is more an enlightenment encouraging a transformation in the learner. The quest for knowledge through learning is unavoidable and potentially very powerful. Immanuel Kant argued that we can only have knowledge of things that are possible to experience.

We generally believe that learning is elevated with experience, awareness, agility and insight. Yet, there is a world of difference between identifying lessons (hindsight) and applying them. All too often, inquiries and post-incident reports are greeted with the refrain that mistakes have been acknowledged and lessons will be learnt.

Translating lessons through a learning process into meaningful actions, however, is sometimes hard and painful, and often requires imagination and transformation: as already mentioned, a failure of imagination is a common refrain in post-incident reporting. Success can confer resilience. This is why it is important to have a system in place that records and transfers lessons—in effect, contributes to a collective memory. As mentioned previously, having a repository to which novice employees can be directed, and from which they can learn what pitfalls to avoid, is worth its weight in gold.

Turning attention to communication, and the use of language (including body language), there is a rich stream of philosophical thinking to offer ideas and guidance. Philosophically, communication refers to the process of intellectual discourse between individuals or groups, resulting in the transmission and interchange of information, experiences, affections, goods and services. A fundamental element of human existence and language is the means of delivery of both knowledge and experience; language brings culture into the equation. Communication informs, directs and persuades. To be effective, the listener must not only get the message but also interpret the message in the way the sender intended. Since communication requires effort, it should always have a purpose: if the purpose is not clear, problems will follow.

A proponent of open dialogue, Socrates would undoubtedly encourage face-to-face communication as the best way to build community, consensus and trust. The Stoics emphasised the importance of reason and self-control which teaches individuals to acknowledge their emotions without being controlled by them when communicating. It also promotes adopting an open mind, being an active listener and showing a willingness to consider other perspectives. [164] Communication involves listening and asking questions. Here, the power behind asking the right question to elicit the best answer does not solely or even significantly reside with the interrogator but also on the listener's ability to respond in a meaningful way.[165]

While technology has increased the speed and frequency of our communication, it is no substitute for direct communication to convey meaning. Communication's modern sense as a reciprocal sharing of minds through dialogue was perhaps best advanced by the philosopher John Locke. He saw communication as the practice by which two or more minds shared ideas with language as the conduit between private meaning and shared understanding. Søren Kierkegaard was one of the first philosophers to make communication a philosophical problem, specifically how to disclose truth amid 'a din of inauthenticity'. This issue resonates today.

The nature and tone of language are key components of communication, and miscommunication too easily occurs when language is imprecise or words are misconstrued. Language can reveal prejudices and biases in the communicator and affect the listener as much as the words used. There is the danger of an echo chamber appearing when words are reflected without meaning or understanding, sometimes because the language used is inappropriate for the audience. Language may also change over time.

A controversial study in the early 1970s introduced a rule that said that 7 per cent of meaning was communicated through spoken word, while 38 per cent came through the tone of voice and 55 per cent through body language: the 7-38-55 rule was developed by Albert Mehrabian from the University of California in his book *Silent Messages* (1972).[166] This distribution, particularly with such a high non-verbal component, may need to be reviewed in the light of social media.

The rapid growth of social media has facilitated the trend where there is often little open dialogue or body language, merely an exchange and reinforcement and similar views courtesy of algorithms. This hollow exchange has been accompanied by a detachment from the norms of civilised conversation with threats and profanities peppering modern dialogue and with little responsibility taken for authorship or deference shown. In many cases, communicators have lost their moral compass and see verbal cruelty as a way of humiliating and demeaning others under a cloak of anonymity rather than having a civil exchange of opposing views. Beyond this, there are many who do not have access to or choose to ignore social media because of the verbal pollution.

In terms of how communication skills can practically influence resilience, a brief consideration of the early testimonies at the COVID-19 pandemic inquiry in the UK reveals some valuable insights. Sir David Spiegelhalter, the chairman of the Winton Centre for Risk and Evidence Communication at the University of Cambridge, testified to the inquiry that the government should adopt in the future a different approach to communicating health risks that: 'treated people with respect'.[167]

He argued that politicians adopted a 'one-sided, manipulative' communications strategy during COVID and thought that they should not deliver public-health messages. He added that: 'The standard government communication is of telling you what to do, either through false reassurance or building up the fears. Both of these [reactions] are deeply untrustworthy, appalling and ineffective.' He added that: 'In trustworthy communication, one of the first things to do is pre-empt misinformation.'

Brooke Rogers, the chair of the UK's Cabinet Office Behavioural Science Expert Group since 2013, has warned against over-reassuring members of the public, particularly about extreme events.[168] The academic and her colleagues from King's College London believe that while reassurance has a role to play, there is a case for understanding public responses on a scale ranging from under-response to over-response. A response at either end of the scale can have potentially detrimental impacts on our ability to respond effectively. The researchers believed that evidence-based, transparent, honest and credible communications were key.

Perception or awareness of the wider world is an important skill for resilience. Being aware of one's self and surroundings allows an individual to judge prospective dangers and risks, thereby permitting avoidance or mitigations. Awareness is about planning rather than a file full of plans: as Dwight Eisenhower once said: 'Plans are worthless but planning is everything.'[169] Politicians can easily mis-appreciate public perceptions in a crisis. They can struggle with communicating uncertainty and potential changes in policy as evidence builds—witness the concatenation of government pronouncements during

COVID-19—'because they are fundamentally different to the vision and direction that they hope to set in normal political cycles'.[170]

Reliance on physical solutions and technologies is generally favoured over reliance on behaviours yet it is the latter which is likely to bring about the required change: if resilience is to be improved, effort and resources should be placed here, particularly ahead of another pandemic.

Philosophers distinguish between accounts which assume that perceptions of objects or beliefs about them are aspects of an individual's mind and those accounts which constitute real aspects of the world external to the individual.[171] The philosophy of perception is mainly concerned with the latter. Many of the traditional puzzles of perception have arisen, for example, when people tried to make sense of the fact that in different circumstances the same things appeared differently, either to different people placed differently or to the same person on different occasions. Such ancient puzzles were fuelled as the scientific revolution developed. Philosophers such as Galileo, Descartes and Locke attempted to make sense of the relationship between perceptual experience and the physical world.

Here, the distinction between internal and external perception will be discussed in terms of self-awareness and situational awareness respectively. Many philosophers down the ages have discussed the realm of awareness or perception and the consequences of their application based on virtues and moral principles. A form of philosophy called situational ethics takes into account the particular context of an act when evaluating it ethically rather than judging it only according to absolute moral standards. The Stoics would say that it is best to allow events to happen since we have little control over them anyway but should be prepared for the consequences.

Self-awareness is a personal attribute or mindset that comes with maturity and experience. It is the conscious reflection of one's own character and feelings, one's strengths and weaknesses, hopefully aligned with one's personal values and aspirations. It allows us to see things from the perspective of others, practise self-control, work creatively and productively, and experience pride in ourselves and our work as well as general self-esteem. A person with a resilient mindset is characterised by a capacity to understand themselves and quickly learn from others, as well as an ability to navigate complex challenges to achieve a purpose that matters to them. Achieving this capacity requires honest self-analysis and introspection. Questioning old patterns of behaviour and asking the crucial 'what can I do better?' rather than 'why did I do this?' can help self-reflection.[172] These are all elements that contribute to making a person resilient.

In his book *The 7 Habits of Highly Effective People* (2020), Stephen Covey claims that: 'Every human has four endowments—self-awareness, conscience, independent will, and creative imagination. These give us the ultimate human freedom...The power to choose, to respond, to change.'[173] These capabilities reinforce resilience. Lack of self-awareness on the other hand can be a significant handicap in leadership. Research has found that as executives climb the corporate ladder, they often become more self-assured and confident. On the downside, they tend to become more self-absorbed and less likely to consider the perspectives of others.[174]

Situational awareness tells us about the world outside our bodies. It is a valuable skill that is acquired through curiosity in the space we inhabit and the people around it. Such awareness is sometimes referred to as horizon-scanning—a form of external monitoring—the extent of the horizon depending on the nature of the enquiry and the time component. Situational awareness has been recognised as a critical yet often elusive foundation for successful decision-making across a broad range of situations. Furthermore, inadequate situational awareness has been identified as one of the primary factors in accidents attributed to human error. This shows that situational awareness can help identify issues before negative consequences materialise.

To be situationally aware consists of drawing a mind map to understand where you are, what is surrounding you, and what challenges lie ahead. This approach allows you to know exactly what is going on around you, so you can come up with a coping strategy. Take the simple example of going for a walk and deciding on what you should wear for inclement weather. As a first step, you need to seek and receive the relevant information on the weather forecast for the day (perception), then interpret the relevant information for your area (comprehension) before deciding on the type of clothes to wear (projection) based on the probable best or worst case. These three steps make situational awareness a deliberate and conscious act that calls for a degree of decision-making and visualisation; it also involves communication should others be involved.[175]

By pursuing such a stepped approach, it reduces the fear (of getting wet!) and increased one's resilience (if it does!). The process can be made highly complicated in some domains such as engineering and safety systems. For instance, a paper titled 'Impact of situational awareness attributes for resilience assessment of active distribution networks using hybrid dynamic Bayesian multi-criteria decision-making approach' is recommended for serious research students.[176] On another level, situational awareness has been shown to improve the resilience management of computer networks.

With situational awareness, it is possible to gain a sense of detachment. This enables the situation to be analysed objectively and to identify opportunities from the choices available. We can develop a resilient mindset that empowers us to learn new survival skills from the challenges we face.[177] Some propose that mindfulness training can help to develop situational awareness (mindful acceptance) of an individual beyond a mind focused on 'what' we want to achieve, into a mind constantly engaged in updating 'how' to achieve it, given the evolving situation (mindfulness competence).[178]

It is claimed that this may help military commanders making wise decisions in chaotic circumstances instead of just reacting to events. By being present and fully engaging with the here and now, it is possible to understand ourselves better and our responses to external circumstances. This mindfulness practice aligns with the Stoic emphasis on self-awareness and control over one's reactions.

The last, but perhaps most important, of the skill set is the social (people) skill. Resilience is, in essence, about people and their interactions. All the infrastructures or technologies in the world, albeit having their own intrinsic resilience, will not make a corporation, community or country more resilient unless the people on the ground, who are the often first responders, can muster themselves into a cohesive force in a reasonably responsive timeframe. The degree of social interactions on the street is a common feature of moral and political discussion among philosophers, political scientists and sociologists.

For the purpose of this chapter and its primary theme of resilience, we will consider three aspects of people and their social engagements that impinge directly on the topic, namely groups (and teams), communities, and governance (including leadership). Underpinning all three, are the fundamental social skills—empathy, active listening, self-awareness, effective communication, and problem-solving—because they enable us to understand and connect with one another at a deeper level. (Self-awareness and communication have been discussed already.) They also help us navigate conflicts, express ourselves effectively, and build positive relationships. By honing these skills, we can enhance our emotional resilience and self-worth which helps to maintain an optimistic outlook. The resilient individual utilises social skills, trust, initiative and motivation to grasp the potential.

Most people gain both emotional and physical support from belonging to a social group: that may be a gang, a club, a sports team, a church or mosque, a work unit or department, etc. The group may even be formed after a trauma or crisis when solace comes through sharing emotions. Some groups require a form of initiation or formal membership rites to strengthen social commitment. Effective bonding with like-minded individuals is important and will increase the level of mutual trust and support, hence the degree of resilience of the group as a whole.

It may also lead to an unhealthy alliance between the members that sponsors violence and generates fear, both within and without. Social belonging involves sharing personal experiences, mutual empathy, common goals and a sense of being connected in a meaningful way. It is therefore a two-way process.

Social skills are essential if a group or team is to function effectively. Collaboration and cooperation require mutual understanding, a degree of compromise, and a common sense of unity of purpose coupled with a desire to problem-solve. A heavy dose of humility and respect will help establish trust, the keystone of any high-performance group. These are the soft skills spoken of earlier. Depending on the nature of the task and group, it may be that the leading and contributing roles may change between participants at any time. That is one of the tenets of a 'self-organising team', one of the staples of an agile philosophy and critical for any collaborative conversation.

The importance of social skills has come more to the fore since COVID-19. The ambiguities and inexactitudes around social resilience in the face of the pandemic have challenged policies and reputations equally if not more than the traditional physical risks. The issue is that the social dimension of resilience is nearly impossible to quantify, forecast or include in any open risk register. According to Chris Needham-Bennett: 'The list of [people] who have fallen foul of the law or the judgement of society is long and ranges from authors to business leaders, [chief financial officers], academics, TV personalities, pundits and of course politicians across the political spectrum.'[179] So, the necessity of social skills applies at all levels and is the foundation of effective teamwork.

When it comes to communities, the scale of social skilling shifts up a gear in order to cater for more disparate groups, often with different perspectives and aims—more so than with tightly knit and usually smaller teams. A community could be a civic grouping, a loose collection of experts or the various departments of a corporation. While sharing broadly common interests or goals, they may diverge in the routes to success and may tend to congregate in silos to defend their respective positions. Social skills need to be more attuned to developing social capital that allows cooperative working and mixing. Here, negotiation between the parties, conflict resolution and empathy for different views are key skill elements.

If successful, they can make the difference between a community surviving through trauma or a disaster or not. According to a post-COVID-19 report: 'Communities have shown that they are one of the most effective elements of disaster and emergency relief. All our resilience planning should include efforts to build up social capital and community infrastructure that can be flexibly deployed at times of crisis.'[180] Hence, no city, company or country can be resilient and enduring if its people do not form the common bond that comes from mixing and working together through communities.

Governments recognise the value of social capital in resilience and are increasingly referring to a whole-of-society or whole-of-nation approach. Developing this is perhaps the ultimate social skill for a country and its collective communities. It could involve millions of citizens, and COVID-19 proved that may be the scale necessary to overcome a threat that potentially affects the whole population. Few countries have developed the civil protective organisation, resources and skills to be able to command and control such a large undertaking.

This leads to the final element of social skilling for a resilience mindset. That is governance, and especially leadership. How we direct and oversee an enterprise of whatever size will largely determine whether it fails or succeeds. Those who govern need to show that they can rise to the multiple and sometimes concurrent challenges by proving a vision—that north star—that both unites and motivates. The skills required are often unique to the set of circumstances as one form of governance or leadership will suit one situation but not another. Leadership needs to evolve and change if resilience is to be ensured.

Take the COVID-19 pandemic and the move to hybrid working that has arisen since. As leaders and managers of organisations now face dealing with people who appear in the office for part of the week, governance skills need to adapt to oversee a distant and disparate workforce. Team and corporate spirit is made more difficult to sustain, and managers may need to pay closer attention to morale and well-being than hitherto. Agglomeration may have its benefits such as making the sharing of skills easier but atomisation is here to stay in working practices so new approaches are needed.

Direction in war also requires different skill sets to govern in peace. Lack of time and resources with an approaching enemy all dictate an urgency that requires less consultation and social niceties. The tendency may be towards authoritarianism but even here consideration of the soldiers' welfare and morale is important for winning. One of the world's great military leaders, Marcus Aurelius, 'governed by absolute power under the guidance of wisdom and virtue', according to the historian Edward Gibbon. [181] Without exerting these virtues, it is all too easy for a lack of governance to tip into anarchy or, more likely, into tyranny and undo the good initially sought. The attributes of a resilient individual can be summarised by the acronym ARC, representing armour, resistance and courage.[182]

Good governance and sound leadership are skill sets that can be learned or coached. The military does it all the time with their early cohorts. Governance is a social skill as it is about inspiring, encouraging and empowering, as well as having a positive, trusting and worthy attitude. Yet, none of this can be effective if the ability to communicate with clarity and focus is weak or absent. Inarticulacy may be a common human failing but a lack of words should not limit the search to find other ways to connect and harmonise. Resilient leaders must also recognise their strengths and weaknesses but can compensate the latter with the former without it being obvious to observers. Rather, the leader must appear competent while conveying that important dose of charisma.

Besides individual and group values, the 'Social Change Model of Leadership' recognises a further category which is termed social/community values.[183] It describes, under the heading of citizenship, the 'process whereby the individual and the collaborative group become responsibly connected to the community and the society through the leadership experience.' Corporate societal responsibility (CSR) reflects a wider world view whereby managers and leaders consider holistically the many diverse components of their respective organisations, including the natural environment, when formulating their resilience strategies. In simple terms, this can be expressed by the popular phrase of 'all for one, one for all'.

The idea is not new, however. Inherent in the Stoic concept of *sympatheia* is the notion of an interconnected cosmos in which everything in the universe is part of a larger whole. Marcus Aurelius was one of the early writers to articulate the notion of cosmopolitanism, saying that he was a citizen of the world not just of Rome. This reflects the interdependency of activities which if ignored can be bad for all and diminish resilience. In *Meditations*, he writes: 'That which is not good for the beehive, cannot be good for the bees.' A good leader understands this mindset and will strive for a collegiate, cohesive approach to problem-solving—and ultimately, satisfaction if not happiness for the greatest number of people. As Aurelius said: 'Very little is necessary for living a happy life…It is all within yourself, in your way of thinking.'[184]

Chapter 9
Sojourn

It isn't the things themselves that disturb people but the judgements that they form about them.
— Epictetus

If resilience is a journey, not a destination, this is the time to have a pit stop or sojourn to take stock of the road travelled so far and see what has been learnt in this philosophical journey of resilience. The aim of this book has not been to review past or present philosophies connected to the topic but to see how ideas and concepts fit with the modern mindset and what points can be drawn from them to improve our resilience mindset for the future. As the philosopher Søren Kierkegaard advises: 'It is really true what philosophy tells us, that life must be understood backwards. But with this, one forgets the second proposition, that it must be lived forwards.' [185] In modern parlance, reviewing the past is like using the rear-view mirror in a car; it is good to glance back occasionally and see how far you have come but if you stare too long you may not see the truck coming towards you: an accident is likely to ensue!

This notwithstanding, there is little that has not already been experienced by our ancestors, and while 'history rarely repeats itself, but its echoes never go away',[186] there is much we can learn by glancing occasionally in that rear-view mirror. The Hellenistic period of two millennia ago presented citizens with a turbulent external and internal environment. It was violent, brutal and unstable: politics were in disarray and disputes abounded. Such turmoil has continued down the ages and extended across nearly every continent.

As Alexis de Tocqueville perceptively wrote in the mid-nineteenth century: 'The world that is arising is still half entangled in the debris of the world that is falling, and in the midst of the immense confusion that human affairs present, no one can say what will remain standing of aged institutions and old mores and what of them will in the end disappear.'[187] Those words have resonance with the twenty-first century. Despite the historical turbulence, philosophers down the ages have given us ideas which have survived interrogation. Collectively, they have presented us with ever more refined and defined philosophical -isms that connect with the modern era. While the use of the term resilience has not been commonplace, many ideas have embodied that concept in one way or another, and drawing them out has been the aim of this book.

By way of a summary of the resilience journey undertaken, this final chapter looks at eight milestones that together represent the distance travelled and the distance to go. Certain key lessons for a resilient mindset can be identified with each milestone.

Milestone #1. Develop your inner strength, deploying virtues and values that strengthen your moral compass while keeping external turbulence and social dislocation in perspective.

The Stoic philosophers set us on a clear path of appreciating wisdom and understanding knowledge as cornerstones of our resilience. They realised that as individuals who cannot significantly influence external events, we should look inward but not with indifference or callousness. This chimes with the philosophy of mindfulness. As resilience is essentially about people and how they work together at the grassroots on restoration and regeneration, the emphasis and effort should be directed there. This is not to dismiss the role of higher authorities such as governments, local authorities or company executives.

They have the rightful and appointed role of casting policies and directing resources overall. But the real success of resilience will be found through individuals and groups coming together to preserve their homes, businesses and communities from disruption. Even a global pandemic like COVID-19 relied on individual preventative measures such as masks and isolation until a vaccine arrived. Individual efforts, taken together, can make a difference. As John O'Donoghue made clear we each can pay our own small part; together it makes the greater whole. Resilience gives us hope of making a positive difference.

A re-examination of the classical virtues and values, the core of much of Western (and some Eastern) philosophy, needs to be reinvigorated because we are struggling to retain our societal footing—and collective resilience—in slippery times. So slippery has it become that some critics question whether we are in danger of losing not only those traditional virtues and values but also our vision for the greater good, and our humanity along the way. The end of the rules-based order around the world has coincided with a weakening of the universality of human rights and associated international norms.

The signs are all too evident: increasing numbers killed or injured in conflicts, particularly innocent civilians; growing incidents of murder, rape or abuse of women in domestic as well as foreign arenas; the wilful torment and violence perpetrated by angry individuals and unscrupulous criminal enterprises, both online and offline; increasing mass migration from unstable regions; and, last but not least, the increasing levels of corruption and cronyism in our various systems of authority. These trends naturally exacerbate our underlying fears which can weaken our resilience—and hope—if not confronted and contradicted.

At the same time, we are becoming inured to the travesties by not only the frequency of the reporting on our electronic screens but also the feeling of physical separation from the worst of the events. Our national and global institutions and standards, based on liberal democracy, are proving insufficient to deal with the unfolding disorder. To put it mildly, and to coin a phrase, there is a 'democratic recession'—to add to the 'recession of the spirit'—underway, and we need new serving suggestions to get through the moral and physical morass. Philosophical reflections and a resilience mindset can help in part to forge a new normal that challenges the debasements.

While maintaining a hopeful but realistic outlook can ease the journey, much more needs to be done collectively to stop 'the fish rotting from the head down', as the proverb warns.

Besides looking inward, there are some positive signs to cling to beyond. Global average life expectancy has more than doubled since the eighteenth century with child mortality at an all-time low, and deaths from diseases like smallpox and leprosy have fallen away in the past half-century. The global literacy rate among adults increased by almost a fifth in the past four decades (albeit dropped across the OECD countries in the past four years) while there are fifty million more girls in school in 2022 than eight years previously.[188] Advances in science and technology have played a large part in this progression but, nonetheless, we struggle with matching the expectations of a growing global population with finite resources and nativist politics that believe they have preference and priority.

Being resilient is admittedly just one part of the coping equation. As the challenges facing humanity grow ever larger, and we struggle in the face of them then resilience can help us to adapt to the changes while we contemplate and prevaricate over precise solutions. Adaptation, along with optimism, is key to facing our fears and eliciting our responses. The climate crisis epitomises this and will demand fundamental, behavioural change in all individuals if the human race is to survive into and beyond the next millennia.

The Stoics believed universal reason and wisdom permeate all of nature and so they sought to live rationally and virtuously in alignment with the natural order. They thought that by structuring lifestyle choices to match nature it could generate tranquillity and thereby happiness. Focusing on what we can influence and foregoing what we cannot control is the essence of mindfulness. We can try to adopt and apply this notion today even with the hurdles in front.

Milestone #2. Deepen relationships for better social interdependence so as to achieve the greater good for the whole of society.

Attitudinal, behavioural or cultural change is not easy, especially for large and traditional communities or populations, and takes time. It requires a wholescale, whole-of-society approach. The Greco-Roman empire may have had centuries to think and adjust, but we have only decades as the natural order is in danger of breaking down in front of us.

The Western trend towards individualism based on individual rights and freedoms, never mind the growth in protectionism and nativism on the larger canvas, presents immense challenges to holism. While we live in an interconnected and interdependent world, with existential threats that are truly international, we find it difficult to adopt that altruistic approach. There are two possible ways forward.

The first is to encourage and collectivise individual efforts which while miniscule in the grander scheme can make a collective difference: the 'confluence of connectedness'. We see this in voluntary, charity and philanthropic projects which can have a significant impact on the ground. Regrettably, officials are sometimes content to over-rely on the voluntary sector to fill a visible gap in policy and resourcing.

The other is to see transformation as a way forward to achieve resilience. The transformation of the caterpillar into the butterfly (metamorphosis) in the natural world provides a window into the nature of resilience in the human world. Through hardship and difficulties, the aggregation of individual parts (whether cells, creatures, citizens or communities) can transform a situation much more in unison than separately. The Roman Emperor Marcus Aurelius recognised this in his notion of 'mutually intertwined movements' that can run deep and wide.

There is a place for both collectivism and transformation in resilience. They can each play a part depending on the circumstances and urgency of the situation. Yet, both demand a level of leadership and vision to achieve a common goal and identity. The Stoic philosophers acknowledged these requirements by talking about social connectedness and the need for change. Yet, there seems to be a current deficit of leadership in many quarters, particularly political. It may be too much to place the burden of finding solutions on certain key individuals—they have all our human failings—but it reinforces the need for better global governance (rather than government) through social connectedness and mutual responsibility around issues that affect us all. This does not detract from localism where that is appropriate: centralism and localism are not necessarily mutually exclusive.

Milestone #3. By focusing on resilience rather than risk it is possible to lessen our fears of uncertainty and change.

People need resilience mindsets and founding philosophies to help rationalise and contextualise their ways of coping with shocks and stresses. The openness and willingness to grasp those ideas and change can be made easier if undertaken in a period of calm and contemplation. Frequently, however, adaptation is undertaken at speed and duress while going through hardship caused by a crisis or traumatic experience. The stress of the situation, and accompanying fear of any imminent change, can lead either to paralysis or precipitate action.[189]

It can also lead to an atomisation of communities and political parties. This can in turn result in a weakening of liberal democracies. As the presenter of the *2023 Reith Lecture* warned: both the 'sirens of authoritarian populism at home and the cynicism of autocratic despots' abroad can undermine the resilience of liberal democracy which relies on the creativity of people, their empowerment and their willing application on the ground.[190]

Because philosophers, or anyone for that matter, are unable to foresee the future with any clarity—there are too many 'known unknowns' and 'unknown unknowns' in Rumsfeldian parlance—then resilience to accelerating change and disorder is our best tool in the toolbox. Resilience gives us options to deploy both mitigation and adaptation, namely ways of reducing the causes of harm and ways of dealing with the consequences. If, for instance, we are approaching the tipping point of restraining climate change to 1.5°C, as many foretell, we need to find better ways and means of coping with both carbon reduction (mitigation) and carbon capture (adaptation). Beyond the technicalities, we should apply ideas that manage our fears, are founded and built on common virtues and values, and recognise that advice, again from Marcus Aurelius, of a 'universal soul'.[191]

The climate emergency is a universal problem, as was COVID-19 and grand designs based on fundamental principles are called for. In the face of uncertainty and the difficulty of planning, precise risk models and reasonable worst-case analysis need to be preceded by broad resilience approaches that can manage the sheer scale of the change pending.

Unprecedented change in the modern world has meant that we have fewer historical reference points to assess future events and hence gauge probabilities with any accuracy. As a result, there is a growing case for turning away from traditional risk-management models and looking at threat-neutral or threat-agnostic approaches that give preference to dealing with the consequences rather than the causes. This is more a resilience management issue. The shift in thinking will not be easy or readily grasped as traditions are always hard to surrender. The risk-industrial complex has a strong hold on our mindset but is increasingly found wanting in our precarious world of trials and tribulations. The philosophy of Ockham's Razor around simplicity has much to recommend in finding the right path through the morass.

Milestone #4. The prepared mind and body require perceptive, persuasive and holistic thinking that can be transformed from a grand vision into sound practical approaches.

Strategies need long-term visions as resilience cannot be generated quickly. They also need planning, preparation, resourcing and commitment. This means that people and organisations need to prioritise sustainable goals over short-term gains. If those goals are all-embracing, involving all parties and stakeholders, and founded around sound cultural and ethical values, they can be transformative with lasting impact. The parties involved in a joint vision will be empowered and enriched. Yet, it demands good leadership and stewardship from people with curiosity, imagination and agility.

In government, application can be helped by cross-party political agreement beyond one-term parliaments as well as proper funding from treasuries to ensure resource longevity and redundancy. This is neither radical science nor perverse philosophy. Yet, it seems hard to achieve in a time of fractious politics.

The animal and plant kingdoms are good at applying survival strategies which is why they have evolved over millennia to occupy almost every niche on the planet. The biological world has been at the resiliency game for much longer than people and many creatures have thrived through tumultuous, evolutionary times. Remarkably, they have done this without planning, predicting or trying to perfect their responses to complex risks. Rather, they simply adapt to solve the challenges they continually face by adopting strategies that are agile and responsive.[192] (See *Nature's Resilience* (2025)).

For our human world, an effective resilience strategy requires both top-down and bottom-up approaches. On the ground, where resilience will come into its own, it is important for officials and executives to offer guidance on personal resilience, empower people where possible, stimulate voluntary service, and encourage community activities. In the echelons of power, it amounts to assembling coalitions of the willing or group-issue networks. If a whole-of-society approach to resilience is to gain traction, it needs to combine solutions up and down the network. Hopefully, they will combine in the middle through the right level of coordination and cooperation.

Promoting the right cause and providing the appropriate level of motivation will be crucial if the numbers involved are to match the potential scale of any systemic crisis. This is easier said than done but sound leadership, good statecraft and the delivery of 'how' rather than 'why' will become ever more the determinant of success.

Milestone #5. Truth and trust can bind people together in a robust social contract and social cohesion that facilitate resilience in the round.

A resilient approach will be largely dependent on the trust between people and officials in authority. Again, COVID-19 tested this aspect of crisis management and was found wanting in many respects. Trust relies in good measure on the truth that is circulated and, conversely, on the untruth or post-truth that is propagated. Social media can be both a benefit and a hindrance; it can spread the truth and disguise the untruth; it can both unite and polarise; it can dampen concerns yet heighten fears. There is growing evidence to indicate that polarisation and mistrust are connected, with the consequence that often the majority do not feel their best interests are being served by political representatives with hardline views.

Trust allows truth to flourish and both can be generated through shared knowledge and commitment from respected organs of power. The *2023 Edelman Trust Barometer* shows that business institutions are more trusted than government or the media: 62 per cent for business compared to 50 per cent for either government or media. In fact, the barometer showed that the institutional leaders most trusted are scientists with coworkers, neighbours and people in the local community all receiving high scores. This underlines the point that trust—generating resilience—can be found and stimulated at the grassroots level. Both trust and truth are fragile.

If the current social fabric is to be repaired and any social contract to be implemented, those in authority need to tap into this zone and communicate with answers to ground-level questions not just give answers to high-level concerns. Enabling populations to become resilient beyond top-down strategies, protocols and standards is a key role of government. One of the most influential aspects of Aristotelian philosophy has been the enabling view of the state, the idea that the function of the state is to make possible the development and well-being of the individual but only by being a member of society can an individual contribute to that fulfilment. This is about societal resilience facilitated by a political commitment to ensure an open and free society.

The key ingredient for societal resilience is social cohesion. The *Khan Review* (2024) has rightly identified social cohesion as an important aspect of a nation's well-being and democratic norms and encouraged a strategic approach to developing social cohesion as part of a national resilience plan. If nurtured, social cohesion can help to deliver a range of positive benefits for society as a whole.

Milestone #6. Change can be an engine of progress but requires agility and adaptation to operate in partnership if resilience rather than resistance is to shine through.

The world about us is changing at what seems an alarming and accelerating rate. The words volatile, uncertain, complex and ambiguous—commonly referred to by the acronym

VUCA—remain as pertinent and potentially pernicious today as when the collective term was introduced in 1987. There is no reason to think that the future will be any different, except for change gaining an ever-faster pace. The impermanence of the universe has been a focus of philosophical debate for millennia.

Yet, increasingly, the patterns of the past are no longer good indicators of the future simply because the pace and pervasiveness of change today are of different orders of magnitude. At the same time, history proves that people of whatever race or creed, and whatever era, have essentially the same fears and emotions, ambitions and motives—frequently making the same mistakes and poor judgements. Hence, we must not ignore the historical lessons but use them wisely to tread a better road ahead.

The two greatest assets to cope with change are agility and adaptiveness. They can work in tandem but require nurturing through the use of techniques such as empowerment, delegation, redundancy, reorganisation and, of course, the deployment of technology. In evolutionary philosophy, Charles Darwin reminds us that species evolve and adapt to changing environments, with natural survival depending not on the fittest but on those who can adapt the fastest to change. This philosophy can be extended to other domains, thereby emphasising the importance of adaptability for survival and growth.

Milestone #7. The meta-skills (i.e., knowledge, communication, perception, people) will play an ever-increasing role in shaping the resilience mindset.

The new demands of the world of work will require many to undertake upskilling and reskilling several times in their lives. This will require the learning of both hard and soft skills. The green revolution, for instance, will demand more car-servicing technicians with battery expertise while behavioural change will be needed to promote a wider circular economy. Technologies will both help and hinder. The growth of artificial intelligence, quantum technologies and cloud computing will potentially provide rich seams of productivity and forecasting. There are also downsides to consider.

They will require some redeployment of jobs and can reduce resilience by forcing a greater dependency on those very technologies that necessitate change. They will also need careful ethical management. The more complex and networked a system, the greater the prospect of disruption. All this change places an added importance on anticipation (foresight) and preparation (prevention), as well as training and exercising to understand the consequences if that preparation proves inadequate and adaptation (insight) becomes necessary.

The trend will also require soft meta-skills around better learning of new knowledge and of past lessons, better communication in all its forms, greater awareness and improved people management. These aspects have been discussed by philosophers over millennia. They are therefore not new, but they have added urgency because of the sheer scale and speed of change in today's world and the urgency of the challenges we currently and collectively face.

Milestone #8. Look back to look forward.

In looking back at philosophical ideas, one cannot help but be impressed by the thinking of those early Greco-Roman characters who saw clearly the fundamentals of human values and aspirations. Quotations from their time pepper our current discussions, whether in managerial guides or through home practices. They saw resilience in the context of personal attitudes as external events were beyond individual control. That notwithstanding, leadership traits and organisational skills were not beyond their remiss. They understood that political and state governance influenced the resilience of society, and societal behaviours were crucial to overcoming major challenges.

Subsequent philosophers have refined their ideas. The concepts they have generally espoused are about people, their attitudes to life and their mindsets. As the German philosopher Martin Heidegger (d.1976) commented: 'We are ourselves the entities to be analysed.' The common recognition is that society is in a state of perpetual change, the pace of which is accelerating inexorably.

While history can give us markers, never repeating itself precisely, what we must do is manage the process of endless change going forward, and this means perpetual problem-solving. That should be focused less on striving for perfection and certainty—both unattainable, as Karl Popper remarked—but on building resilience to the inevitable shocks and stresses.

The 'open society' that Popper advocated as an effective approach to problem-solving is facing real strain in today's troubled and turbulent times.[193] The philosopher, writing in

1945, warned of the dangers inherent in centrally planned political systems and attacked the philosophies of Plato, Hegel and Marx. Some would argue that Popper's warnings are being forgotten as modern democracies come under strain with parties and politicians who want to concentrate power under nativistic flags. The right to defend oneself against all comers is a popular message but can be a slippery slope to using any means available to achieve so-called victory under the guise of vitriol or vengeance. We should therefore look back to see forward more clearly.

The less manageable the issues become, whether local, national or international, the more resilient we should strive to be. This is true for citizens, communities, corporations and countries alike. Resilience will allow us to bounce back and forward, whatever the crisis. Our resilience should be generic and not geared to one particular crisis as new, unexpected challenges will surely cross our paths, either sequentially or concurrently.

Yet, resilience needs nurturing as it is not necessarily an inherent state. This effort is part of the ongoing battle for democracy. The *Bertelsmann Stiftung's Transformation Index* (2024) concludes that: 'In the defence of democracy, one crucial stronghold is the resilience of civil society.'[194]

We all have a role to play here in balancing self with society. It is more than having spare batteries in the house should the lights fail; it is about reinventing our whole approach and adapting our behaviours to anticipate the next change that is coming down the road, lights or no lights. As the Stoics recommended, it is about looking back, forwards and inside ourselves all at the same time. Sometimes, we need to look with fresh eyes. The French novelist Marcel Proust (d.1922) expressed it well: 'The only true voyage of discovery…would be not to visit strange lands but to possess other eyes.'[195]

Hopefully, this book has offered some insights into the resilience mindset. In conclusion, and unapologetically, the words of the philosopher Søren Kierkegaard should ring in our ears and help to keep us focused on the winding road ahead. There is hope there: 'It is better to travel hopefully than to arrive.'[196]

Other Books

Building Resilient Futures (2023)

ISBN: 9781035812622

Whether a community struggling to keep its members buoyant, a business trying to stay solvent, or a nation fighting to protect its citizens, adversity and crisis impact us all. The resilient can pick themselves up, dust themselves off, and not only bounce back but also bounce forward.

This book looks at what resilience means in times of crisis as well as the in-between periods. It examines the various types of resilience, such as emotional, organisational and societal, and offers valuable insights on how to manage the consequences of upheaval and trauma.

The author brings together contributors to deliver a real mix of theory, case-study evidence and anecdote in a way that is both approachable and thought-provoking. It is a timely and necessary addition to a crucial topic. Very simply, professionals, practitioners, students, government ministers, and business leaders should read this now. It might be a safer, better world if people read the book and acted on it.

'Passionate, persuasive and a wake-up call to national resilience complacency. This is not a 'handbook', it is a grenade tossed into the meandering procrastination of national resilience. A brilliant summary of the enormous challenges of gaining ultimate 'resilience'. Hugely entertaining and challenging. The author's overview of all aspects of resilience broadens the resilience debate to where it should be. At last, an enjoyable 'must read' for anyone involved in the field. Very simply, professionals, practitioners, students, government ministers, and business leaders should read this now. 'A safer, better world?'—it might be if people read the book and act on it.'

'In Building Resilient Futures, the author has found a way to integrate the complexities necessary for businesses and organisations to achieve resilience. It is critical reading for all those who hold responsibility for organisational resilience.'

The Triptych (2024)

ISBN: 9781035830169

This is a historical, semi-biographical novel. It is the story of three remarkable men. They were neither supreme sportsmen nor medical pioneers, without fortunes or titles. Rather, they were ordinary men caught up in three periods of British history—the 1855 Siege of Sebastopol in the Crimean War, the Expedition to rescue General Gordon in 1884–85, and the fierce Dodecanese Campaign in 1943. The prominence of the characters comes from the fact that all three survived their ordeals to reflect the spirit and resilience of their time.

The author creates a fictional work by linking the three characters and their wartime fortunes through an imaginary device, a Russian triptych. This object is handed down from one person to another, eventually hanging on the wall of the house of the author's father. One picture contains the memories of three lifetimes. The real-life medals from all three campaigns currently hang on the author's wall.

THE TRIPTYCH

Robert Hall

Nature's Resilience (2025)

ISBN: 9781035878260

The ways that biological organisms survive and thrive within a changing world can tell us a lot about ourselves, our behaviours and our approach to problem-solving. We may not be able to learn directly from the pine tree, the bear or the octopus, but they can reveal activities, behaviours, even chemicals or genes, that can benefit our world. Moreover, animals and plants have been at the resiliency game for much longer than people and many have thrived through tumultuous, evolutionary times.

They can therefore provide examples of how nature has solved challenges, and we should be humble enough to take note and reflect. The solutions can indeed have relevance for our complex and sophisticated range of human activities such as healthcare and well-being, including the sources of valuable drugs that can alleviate human ailments; physical security and national deterrence; crisis management and business continuity; organisational agility and corporate networking.

This is the third part of the series of books on resilience.

'Robert Hall, with his killer combination of business and zoology, dives into the natural world to show us how much we can learn from our fellow creatures about resilience and how to thrive against the odds. Packed with interest, this book teaches us that lessons from nature are not theoretical they are hard-won, sharpened over millennia on the angle grinder of natural selection. We would do well to listen.'

'Robert Hall's multi-faceted and penetrating analysis of natural resilience is fascinating. He provides a wide range of examples of how it is achieved and delivers timely warnings about natural limits and the tipping points that face all natural systems. There are many lessons for our human existence, including the difficult choices about where we may need to intervene to maintain and restore equilibrium, and where it might be better to leave nature to take its course, through the complex natural processes that have emerged over millions of years and which we are only beginning to understand.'

References

Chapter 1

[1] Dizikes, P. (2011) 'When the butterfly effect took flight', MIT News Magazine.
https://www.technologyreview.com/2011/02/22/196987/when-the-butterfly-effect-took-flight/

[2] Taleb, N. N. (2012) Antifragile: Things That Gain from Disorder, Penguin. ISBN: 0141038225.

[3] Ruff, C., Holt, B., Trinkaus, E. (2006) 'Who's afraid of the big bad Wolff? "Wolff's law" and bone functional adaptation', *American Journal of Physical Anthropology*, 129, 4.
https://onlinelibrary.wiley.com/doi/10.1002/ajpa.20371

[4] 'Our Common Agenda – A Report of the UN Secretary General' (2021).
https://www.un.org/en/content/common-agenda-report/assets/pdf/Common_Agenda_Report_English.pdf

[5] The term 'build back better' was first introduced at the UN Economic and Social Council in July 2005 by former US President Bill Clinton.

[6] 'Hybrid Threats: A comprehensive resilience ecosystem', EU Paper, March 2023. *https://www.hybridcoe.fi/wp-content/uploads/2023/09/JRC129019_02.pdf*

[7] Ibid.

[8] Dweck, C S. (2007) *Mindset: The New Psychology of Success*, Ballantine Books. ISBN: 9780345472328. A summary can be found at: *https://fs.blog/carol-dweck-mindset/*

[9] Bricklin, J. (2015) *The Illusion of Will, Self, and Time: William James's Reluctant Guide to Enlightenment*, SUNY Press. ISBN: 978-1438456270. Quoted in article 'Walking Backward Toward the Future', Bricklin, J. Tricycle, Spring 2017. *https://tricycle.org/magazine/walking-backward-toward-future/*

[10] Vierci, P. (2023) *Society of the Snow*, Constable. ISBN: 1408716372.

[11] Wildavsky, A. (1979) 'Views: No Risk is the Highest Risk of All', *American Scientist*, 67, 32–37. *https://www.jstor.org/stable/27849058*

[12] Seneca, L. A. (2020) *Letters from a Stoic*. Letter 13, 'On Groundless Fears'. *https://thestoicletters.com/seneca-letter-xiii-on-groundless-fears/*

[13] Körner, M. (2022) *Fox and Bear: A Tender Modern Fable About Reversing the Anthropocene.* ISBN: 9780889956469.

[14] According to the OECD's *Programme for International Student Assessment* (PISA), mean performance across OECD countries for 15-year-olds between 2018 and 2022 in mathematics fell by a record 15 points. Reading fell 10 points, twice the previous record, whereas science

performance did not change significantly.
https://www.oecd.org/publication/pisa-2022-results/
[15] 'Ipsos Global Trustworthiness Monitor Report' (2023). https://www.ipsos.com/en/trust
[16] '2024 Edelman Trust Barometer Global Report'. *https://www.edelman.com/trust/2024/trust-barometer*
[17] 'Debate at the Harvard Museum of Natural History', Cambridge, Mass. (USA), 9 September 2009. *https://www.youtube.com/watch?v=N8_W2cBAO7s*

Chapter 2

[18] O'Donohue, J. (2007) *Benedictus*, Transworld Publishers. ISBN: 9780593058626.

[19] Purser, R. (2019) 'The mindfulness conspiracy', *The Guardian*.

[20] Oliver, T. (2020) *The Self Delusion: The Surprising Science of How We Are Connected and Why That Matters*, Weidenfeld & Nicolson. ISBN: 1474611745.

[21] Sherman, N. (2021) *Stoic Wisdom: Ancient Lessons for Modern Resilience*, Oxford University Press. ISBN: 0197501834.

[22] Oliver, T. Ibid.

[23] Pennock, S. F. (2023) 'Who Is Martin Seligman and What Does He Do?' *Positive Psychology*. *https://positivepsychology.com/who-is-martin-seligman/*

[24] Aurelius, M. Ibid, Book 9.

[25] Sherman, N. Ibid

[26] Corbett, J S. (1911) *Some Principles of Maritime Strategy*. *https://www.gutenberg.org/files/15076/15076-h/15076-h.htm*

[27] Oliver, T. Ibid.

[28] Sherman, N. Ibid.

[29] Hall, R. (2023) *Building Resilient Futures*, Austin Macauley Publishers. ISBN: 9781035812622.

[30] Vester, F. (2012) *The Art of Interconnected Thinking*, McB-Verlag, Munich. ISBN: 3939314056.

[31] Shea, J. (2023) Presentation to Risk and Resilience Conference at International Security Expo. *https://resiliencefirst.org/news/ten-lessons-from-the-international-risk-resilience-conference/*

[32] Sherman, N. Ibid.

[33] Zolli, A. and Healy, A. M. (2012) *Resilience: Why Things Bounce Back*, Headline Publishing. ISBN: 9780755360352.

[34] 'How To Be A Great Leader: Timeless Leadership Traits From Roman Emperors, Philosophers, and More', Daily Stoic. *https://dailystoic.com/leadership/*

[35] Calder, G., Calder, K. (2023) *Stoicism at the Summit: Embodying Ancient Principles for Peak Performance and Leadership in Business*. ISBN: 9798866774128.

Chapter 3

[36] Lebell, S. (2007) *Art of Living: The Classical Manual on Virtue, Happiness, and Effectiveness*, HarperOne. ISBN: 9780061286056.

[37] Sharp, H. (2022) 'Spinoza on the Fear of Solitude', *Oxford Studies in Early Modern Philosophy*, 137–162. *https://philarchive.org/rec/SHASOT-16#:~:text=Spinoza%20is%20widely%20understood%20to, and%20universal%20fe ar%20of%20solitude.*

[38] List of phobias. *https://en.wikipedia.org/wiki/List_of_phobias*

[39] According to research by Harvard University, flying in the USA, Europe and Australia is significantly safer than driving a car. Your odds of being in an accident during a flight is one in 1.2 million, and the chances of that accident being fatal are one in 11 million. Your chances of dying in a car crash, conversely, are one in 5,000. *https://theweek.com/97155/fact-check-is-flying-safe*

[40] Peckham, R. (2023) *Fear: An Alternative History of the World*, Profile Books, ISBN: 1788167236.

[41] Clark, C. (2013) *The Sleepwalkers: How Europe Went to War in 1914*, Penguin. ISBN: 0141027827.

[42] De Tocqueville, A. (2003) *Democracy in America*, Volume 2, Part 3, Chapter 11, Penguin Classics. ISBN: 9780140447606.

[43] 'Class of Covid Report 2022', The Prince's Trust. *https://downloads.ctfassets.net/qq0roodynp09/57AtHBpUjeh Ex5JWXsa5ma/59c709ea468ea6a95e4e71c644f6e40b/Class _of_Covid_Report_2022.pdf*

[44] *The Economist*, 9 December 2023.

[45] McCurdy, C. and Murphy, L. (2024) 'We've only just begun', Resolution Foundation report.

*https://www.resolutionfoundation.org/app/uploads/2024/02/
Weve-only-just-begun.pdf*

[46] Massumi, B. (1993) *Politics of Everyday Fear*. University of Minnesota Press. ISBN: 9780816684724. Abstract can be found at:
https://muse.jhu.edu/pub/23/edited_volume/chapter/1262554

[47] Kant, I. (1978) *Anthropology from a Pragmatic Point of View*, Southern Illinois University Press. ISBN: 0809320606.

[48] Svendsen, L. Fr. H. (2008) *The Philosophy of Fear*. ISBN: 9781861894045.

[49] Willyard, C. (2010) 'Fearless Woman Lacks Key Part of Brain', *Science*.
https://www.science.org/content/article/fearless-woman-lacks-key-part-brain

[50] Parmar, R. (2022) 'The science of resilience and wisdom', *Psychiatric Times*, 39, 5.
https://www.psychiatrictimes.com/view/the-science-of-resilience-and-wisdom

[51] Motivational salience is the process that propels an individual's behaviour towards or away from a particular object, perceived event or outcome. It reflects one's risk appetite. See Puglisi-Allegra, S., Ventura, R. (2012) 'Prefrontal/accumbal catecholamine system processes high motivational salience', *Frontiers in Behavioural Neuroscience*, 6, 31.
https://www.ncbi.nlm.nih.gov/pmc/articles/PMC3384081/

[52] Tearle, O. 'Who Said, "We Have Nothing to Fear Except Fear Itself"?' Dispatches from the Secret Library.

https://interestingliterature.com/2020/04/nothing-fear-except-fear-itself-quotation-origin/

[53] 'Letters to a Stoic'. *https://en.wikipedia.org/wiki/Epistulae_Morales_ad_Lucilium*

[54] Seneca, L. Ibid.

[55] Jonas, H. (1984) *The Imperative of Responsibility: In Search of an Ethics for the Technological Age*, University of Chicago Press. ISBN: 9780226405971.

[56] *The Precautionary Principle*. UN Educational, Scientific and Cultural Organisation (UNESCO). World Commission on the Ethics of Scientific Knowledge and Technology (COMEST). Retrieved 2 January 2020. *https://unesdoc.unesco.org/ark:/48223/pf0000139578*

[57] Ferriss, T. (2017) 'Why you should define your fears instead of your goals', TED Talk. *https://www.ted.com/talks/tim_ferriss_why_you_should_define_your_fears_instead_of_your_goals*

[58] Furedi, F. (2018) *How Fear Works: Culture of Fear in the Twenty-First Century*, Bloomsbury Continuum. ISBN: 9781472947727.

[59] van der Helm, R. (2006) 'Towards a clarification of probability, possibility and plausibility: how semantics could help futures practice to improve', *Foresight*, 8, 3, 17–27. *https://cspo.org/wp-content/uploads/2014/11/read_van-der-Helm-Towards-a-Clarification-of-Probability.pdf*

[60] Needham-Bennett, C. (2023) 'The illusion of risk', Resilience First. *https://resiliencefirst.org/news/the-illusion-of-risk/*

[61] Huntington, S P. (1997) *The Clash of Civilizations and the Remarking of World Order*, Simon & Schuster. ISBN: 0684819872.

[62] Devlin, J. (2024) 'Bridging the gap between regulation and private sector innovation', Resilience First. *https://resiliencefirst.org/news/bridging-the-gap-between-regulation-and-private-sector-innovation-event-roundup/*

[63] Roberts, A. (2023) 'From Risk to Resilience: How Economies Can Thrive in a World of Threats', *Foreign Affairs. https://www.foreignaffairs.com/world/risk-resilience-economics*

Chapter 4

[64] Three Treasures (Taoism). *https://en.wikipedia.org/wiki/Three_Treasures_(Taoism)*

[65] Plato. (2007) *The Republic*, The Political Virtues, Book IV, Penguin Classics. ISBN: 9780140455113

[66] 'Stoic virtues: A short introduction to the 4 Stoic virtues'. Updated 27 July 2022. *https://stoicquotes.com/stoic-virtues/*

[67] Parmar, R. Ibid.

[68] *A Revolution in Kindness*, edited by Anita Roddick. ISBN: 0954395913.

[69] Hall, R. Ibid.

[70] Freedman, Sir Lawrence. (2013) *Strategy: A History*, Oxford University Press. ISBN: 0199325154.

[71] 'The 9/11 Commission Report' (2004) *https://www.9-11commission.gov/report/911Report.pdf*

[72] Burke, E. (2020) *Letter to a Member of the National Assembly.* HardPress. ISBN: 9780461912364.

[73] Taleb, N. N. (2018) *Skin in the Game: Hidden Asymmetries in Daily Life*, Random House. ISBN: 9780425284629.

[74] Kipling, R. 'If', Poetry Foundation.
https://www.poetryfoundation.org/poems/46473/if---

[75] Milo, R., Greenspoon, L., Krieger, E., Sender, R. (2023) 'The global biomass of wild mammals', Proceedings of the National Academy of Science of the United States.
https://www.pnas.org/doi/10.1073/pnas.2204892120

[76] Earth Overshoot Day.
https://overshoot.footprintnetwork.org/how-many-earths-or-countries-do-we-need/#:~:text=Humanity%20is%20using%20nature%201.7,the%20resources%20of%201.7%20Earths.

[77] 'Degrowth – what's behind the economic theory and why does it matter right now?' World Economic Forum, 15 June 2022.
https://www.weforum.org/stories/2022/06/what-is-degrowth-economics-climate-change/

[78] McAslan, A. (2011) 'Community resilience: Understanding the Concept and its Application', Discussion Paper, Torrens Resilience Institute (Australia).
https://www.flinders.edu.au/content/dam/documents/research/torrens-resilience-institute/understanding-community-resilience.pdf

[79] Roberts, A. Ibid.

[80] Ibid.

[81] Martin, R L. (2020) *When more is not better: overcoming America's obsession with economic activity*, Harvard Business Review Press. ISBN: 9781647820060.

[82] 'Bertelsmann Stiftung's Transformation Index (BTI) 2024'. *https://bti-project.org/en/press*

[83] 'Income Inequality', IMF, 2022. *https://www.imf.org/en/Topics/Inequality/introduction-to-inequality*

[84] 'Poverty and Inequality Platform', The World Bank. *https://pip.worldbank.org/home*

[85] *The Economist*, 2 August 2022.

[86] 'Gap among and within countries'. (2020) EU Foresight Report. *https://knowledge4policy.ec.europa.eu/foresight/topic/diversifying-inequalities/gap-within-among-countries_en*

[87] *The Economist*, 7 March 2024.

[88] Credit Suisse, 'Global Wealth Report 2022'. *https://www.getabstract.com/en/summary/global-wealth-report-2022/46249*

[89] McAslan, A. Ibid.

[90] EriOlu, O. (2024) 'The UK's 'Resilience Statement' and the implications on the infrastructure sector', Resilience First. *https://resiliencefirst.org/news/the-uks-resilience-statement-and-the-implications-on-the-infrastructure-sector/*

[91] Kim, J. H., Hawley, C. E., Gonzalez, R., Vo, A. K., Barbir, L. A., McMahon, B. T., Lee, D. H., Lee, J. H. and Lee, Y. W. (2017) 'Resilience from a Virtue Perspective', *Rehabilitation Counseling Bulletin*.

https://www.researchgate.net/publication/317575072_Resilience_From_a_Virtue_Perspective

Chapter 5

[92] Aristotle. (2009) *The Nicomachean Ethics*, Book II. Oxford World Classics. ISBN: 9780199213610. For a discussion of Nicomachean Ethics, listen to BBC Sounds, In Our Time, 2 November 2023.
https://www.bbc.co.uk/sounds/play/m001rylh
[93] Syed, M. (2004) 'Locked in by language, we are freed by music, poetry, painting…and love', *The Times*.
[94] Diamond, J. (2019) *Upheaval: How Nations Cope with Crisis and Change*, Allen Lane. ISBN: 9780241003398.
[95] For two management consultants' perspectives, see: McKinsey & Company. (2020) 'More than a mission statement; How the 5Ps embed purpose to deliver value'.
https://www.mckinsey.com/capabilities/strategy-and-corporate-finance/our-insights/more-than-a-mission-statement-how-the-5ps-embed-purpose-to-deliver-value;
Deloitte C-suite insights, (2022), 'How purpose delivers value in every function and for the enterprise'.
https://www2.deloitte.com/us/en/pages/about-deloitte/articles/how-purpose-delivers-value.html
[96] BSI PAS 808: Purpose-Driven Organisations.
https://www.bsigroup.com/en-IN/Standards-and-Publications/pas-808/#:~:text=PAS%20808%3A2022%20is%20a,decisions%2C%20and%20how%20it%20acts.

[97] Brewer, R. (2023) 'It's time to 'rephrase' how companies work', The World Ahead, *The Economist.*

[98] Fink, L. (2018) Letter to CEOs. *https://www.nytimes.com/2018/01/15/business/dealbook/blackrock-laurence-fink-letter.html*; (2022) Letter to CEOs. *https://www.blackrock.com/corporate/investor-relations/larry-fink-ceo-letter*

[99] Sir Andrews, I. (2021) 'Operational resilience: a guide for non-executive directors', Chapter on Stewardship, Resilience First. *https://www.resiliencefirst.org/sites/default/files/2021-07/RF_NEDs_7%20July%202021%20FINAL.pdf*

[100] Baker, C. (2022) 'What are ethical values in business?' *Leaders. https://leaders.com/articles/company-culture/ethical-values.*

[101] *The Guardian*, 5 May 2015.

[102] Kahle, L. R. and Kennedy, P. (1988) 'Using the List of Values (LOV) to Understand Customers', *Journal of Services Marketing*, 2, 3, 29–56. *https://www.researchgate.net/publication/276060836_Using_the_List_of_Values_LOV_to_Understand_Consumers*

[103] Schwartz, S. H. (2012) 'An overview of the Schwartz theory of basic values', *Online Readings in Psychology and Culture*, 2, 1. *https://scholarworks.gvsu.edu/orpc/vol2/iss1/11/*

[104] Southern, M. G. (2022) 'Mark Zuckerberg announces Meta's new company values', *Search Engine Journal. https://www.searchenginejournal.com/mark-zuckerberg-announces-metas-newcompany-values/438298/*

[105] King Charles III. (2023) 'The King's speech at Mansion House'. *https://www.royal.uk/mansion-house*

[106] 'Despite ESG backlash, linking ESG goals to pay may help the planet', IESE Business School, 12 September 2023. *https://www.forbes.com/sites/iese/2023/09/12/despite-esg-backlash-linking-esg-goals-to-pay-may-help-the-planet/*

[107] 'ESG is missing a metric: R for resilience', World Economic Forum, 7 June 2021. *https://www.weforum.org/stories/2021/06/esg-resilience-investment-environment-social-governance/*

[108] EU Corporate sustainability reporting. *https://finance.ec.europa.eu/capital-markets-union-and-financial-markets/company-reporting-and-auditing/company-reporting/corporate-sustainability-reporting_en*

[109] 'World Values Survey Cultural Map 2023'. *https://www.worldvaluessurvey.org/WVSNewsShow.jsp?ID=467*

[110] 'The basic principles of working in Defence', Ministry of Defence, May 2011. *https://assets.publishing.service.gov.uk/media/5a7572d4e5274a1622e21dde/the_basic_principles_of_working_in_defence.pdf*

[111] Quote is attributed to management consultant and writer Peter Drucker.

[112] Hall, R. Ibid.

[113] Brewer, R. Ibid.

[114] Covey, S. R. *The 7 Habits of Highly Effective People*, Simon & Schuster. ISBN: 9781471195204.

[115] *UK Stewardship Code*, Financial Reporting Council, 30 September 2023. *https://www.frc.org.uk/library/standards-codes-policy/stewardship/uk-stewardship-code/*
[116] Sir Andrews, I. Ibid.
[117] '2022 Edelman Trust Barometer'. *https://www.edelman.com/trust/2022-trust-barometer*
[118] World Values Survey. Ibid.
[119] Goodwin, M. (2023) *Values, Voice and Virtue: The New British Politics*, Penguin. ISBN: 9780141999098.

Chapter 6

[120] 'The ethics and epistemology of trust', Internet Encyclopaedia of Philosophy. *https://iep.utm.edu/trust/*
[121] Svendsen, L. Ibid.
[122] Hall, R. (2019) 'Trust is a vital component of resilience', Resilience First. *https://resiliencefirst.org/news/trust-is-a-vital-component-of-resilience/*
[123] Aldrich, D. P. 'The role of social capital and social networks in resilience'. *https://www.researchgate.net/publication/245024251_Building_Resilience_Social_Capital_in_Post-Disaster_Recovery*
[124] Fukuyama, F. (1996) *Trust: The Social Virtues and the Creation of Prosperity*, The Free Press. ISBN: 9780684825250.
[125] Carter, J. A. (2020) 'On Behalf of a Bi-Level Account of Trust', *Philosophical Studies*, 177, 8, 2299-2322. *https://doi.org/10.1007/s11098-019-01311-2*

[126] Carter, A. (2022) 'Trust and trustworthiness', *Philosophical and Phenomenological Research*, 107, 2, 377–394.
https://onlinelibrary.wiley.com/doi/full/10.1111/phpr.12918
[127] Ansell, B. (2023) 'The Reith Lectures 2023', Part 2, Our Democratic Futures. BBC.
https://www.bbc.co.uk/programmes/m001t3cf
[128] Dame Khan, S. (2024) 'The Khan Review: executive summary, key findings and recommendations', UK government.
https://www.gov.uk/government/publications/the-khan-review-threats-to-social-cohesion-and-democratic-resilience/the-khan-review-executive-summary-key-findings-and-recommendations
[129] Kruger, D. (2020) 'Levelling up our communities: proposals for a new social covenant'.
https://www.dannykruger.org.uk/files/2020-09/Kruger%202.0%20 Levelling%20Up%20Our%20 Communities.pdf
[130] 'Government resilience: extreme weather', A Report by the National Audit Office, 6 December 2023. ISBN: 9781786045218.
https://www.nao.org.uk/reports/government-resilience-extreme-weather/
[131] Diviney, R. 'How to develop the 4 elements of trust', *The Attributes*, July 2022. *https://theattributes.com/blog/how-to-develop-the-4-elements-of-trust*
[132] Zenger, J. and Folkman, J. (2019) 'The 3 elements of trust'.
https://hbr.org/2019/02/the-3-elements-of-trust

[133] 'Global Resilience Survey 2023', Control Risks. *https://www.controlrisks.com/-/media/corporate/files/campaigns/global-resilience-survey/global-resilience-report-control-risks.pdf*

[134] '2023 Edelman Trust Barometer', *https://www.edelman.com/trust/2023/trust-barometer*

[135] 'World Economic Forum Global Risks Report 2024'. *https://www.weforum.org/publications/global-risks-report-2024/*

[136] 'The EIT Food Trust Report' (2020). *https://www.eitfood.eu/reports/trust-report-2020*

[137] *Post-truth politics.* https://en.wikipedia.org/wiki/Post-truth_politics

[138] Arendt, H. (2005) 'Truth: engagements across philosophical traditions', *Truth and Politics*, Blackwell. ISBN: 9780470776407.

[139] Barrera, O., Guriev, S., Henry, E., Zhuravskata, E. (2020) 'Facts, alternative facts, and fact checking in times of post-truth politics', *Journal of Public Economics*, 182. *https://www.sciencedirect.com/science/article/pii/S0047272719301859*

[140] Hamel, G. and Zanini, M. (2020) *Humanocracy: Creating Organizations as Amazing as the People*, Harvard Business Review Press. ISBN: 9781633696020.

Chapter 7

[141] Jung, C. G. (2023) *The Structures and Dynamics of the Psyche*, Routledge. ISBN: 9781032603292.

[142] Samuel, J. (2021) *This Too Shall Pass: Stories of Change, Crisis and Hopeful Beginnings*, Penguin. ISBN: 0241348870.

[143] Attributed to Reinhold Niebuhr, Lutheran theologian and philosopher (1892–1971).

[144] Aquinas, St Thomas. (2018) *Summa Theologica*, Coyote Canyon Press. ISBN: 9781732190320.

[145] Fereday, J. (2023) 'Agility: Managing on the edge of chaos', *Philonomist*, 6 June 2023.
https://www.philonomist.com/en/article/agility

[146] Braun, T. J., Hayes, B. C., Frautschy DeMuth, R. L., Taran, O A. (2017) 'The development, validation, and practical application of an employee agility and resilience measure to facilitate organizational change', *Industrial and Organizational Psychology*, 10, 4.
https://www.researchgate.net/publication/321227267_The_Development_Validation_and_Practical_Application_of_an_Employee_Agility_and_Resilience_Measure_to_Facilitate_Organizational_Change

[147] 'Agile resilience in the UK: Lessons from COVID-19 for the "next normal"', McKinsey & Company, 13 October 2020.
https://www.mckinsey.com/capabilities/people-and-organizational-performance/our-insights/agile-resilience-in-the-uk-lessons-from-covid-19-for-the-next-normal

[148] Hall, R. Ibid.

[149] 'The Fukushima Daiichi accident report by the director general'.
https://www-pub.iaea.org/mtcd/publications/pdf/pub1710-reportbythedg-web.pdf

[150] Leroi, A. M. (2015) 'The Lagoon: how Aristotle invented science', Bloomsbury, pp. 91–92, 273, 288. ISBN: 9781408836224.

[151] 'Seatbelt advertising: a journey through the last 50 years', Road Safety GB, 16 April 2018.
https://roadsafetygb.org.uk/news/seatbelt-advertising-a-journey-through-the-last-50-years/

[152] Roberts, A. Ibid.

[153] Cuginotti, A. 'Imaginal cells | the caterpillar's job to resist the butterfly', Butterfly Connection.
https://augustocuginotti.com/imaginal-cells-caterpillars-job-to-resist-butterfly/

[154] Lauritzen, P. (2022) 'A philosopher's guide to messy transformations', *Strategy + Business*. *https://www.strategy-business.com/article/A-philosophers-guide-to-messy-transformations*

[155] 'What is business transformation?' McKinsey & Company, 17 April 2023.
https://www.mckinsey.com/featured-insights/mckinsey-explainers/what-is-business-transformation

[156] Machiavelli, N. (2003) *The Prince*, Chapter 6, Penguin Classics. ISBN: 9780140449150.

Chapter 8

[157] Dweck, C. S. S. Ibid.

[158] Cote, C. (2022) 'Growth mindset vs fixed mindset: What's the difference?' Harvard Business School Online.

https://online.hbs.edu/blog/post/growth-mindset-vs-fixed-mindset

[159] Long, B. 'Hard Skills vs. Soft Skills: What Are They? (With Examples)', *Insight Global*. *https://insightglobal.com/blog/hard-skills-vs-soft-skills/*

[160] Sir Seldon, A. (2023) 'Advocating for character education: Sir Anthony Seldon's call to action for teachers', *Role Models*. *https://www.linkedin.com/pulse/advocating-character-education-sir-anthony-seldons/*

[161] 'The Times Education Commission final report', 15 June 2022. *https://s3.documentcloud.org/documents/22056664/times-education-commission-final-report.pdf*

[162] Commercial Education Trust, 27 January 2022. *https://www.thetimes.com/uk/education/article/times-education-commission-125-billion-a-year-boost-to-economy-cgrgkxs6v*

[163] Ruck, A. (2018) 'The hidden benefits of higher education: mental health and resilience', *Office for Students*. *https://www.officeforstudents.org.uk/news-blog-and-events/blog/the-hidden-benefits-of-higher-education-mental-health-and-resilience/*

[164] 'Communication & Stoicism: How to communicate better with Stoic philosophy', Stoic Simple. *https://www.stoicsimple.com/communication-stoicism-how-to-communicate-better-with-stoic-philosophy/*

[165] Lauritzen, P. (2019) 'What you don't know about questions', TEDxFrederiksberg.

https://www.ted.com/talks/pia_lauritzen_what_you_don_t_k now_about_questions

[166] Mehrabian, A. (1972) *Silent Messages: Implicit Communication of Emotions and Attitudes*, Wadsworth Publishing Company. ISBN: 9780534000592

[167] Hayward, E. (2023) 'Fear-mongering Covid adverts 'appalling and manipulative', *The Times.*

[168] 'Effective communication with the public during a crisis', Roundtable Report, National Preparedness Commission, April 2023.
https://nationalpreparednesscommission.uk/event-summary/effective-communication-with-the-public-during-a-crisis-round-table/

[169] Eisenhower, D. D. (1957) 'Remarks at the National Défense Executive Reserve Conference'.

[170] Ibid.

[171] BonJour, L. (2007) 'Epistemological Problems of Perception', Stanford Encyclopaedia of Philosophy. *https://philpapers.org/rec/BONEPO*

[172] Perry, E. (2022) 'What is self-awareness and how to develop it?' BetterUp. *https://www.betterup.com/blog/what-is-self-awareness*

[173] Covey, S R. Ibid.

[174] Galinsky, A. D., Magee, J. C., Inesi, M. E., Gruenfeld, D. (2009) 'Losing touch', *Kellogg Insight.*
https://insight.kellogg.northwestern.edu/article/losing-touch

[175] Endsley, M. and Jones, D. (2016) *Designing for Situation Awareness* (Second ed.), CRC Press. ISBN: 9781420063585.

[176] Sonal, D. G. (2022) 'Impact of situational awareness attributes for resilience assessment of active distribution networks using hybrid dynamic Bayesian multi criteria decision-making approach', *Reliability Engineering & System Safety*, 228.
https://www.researchgate.net/publication/363034319_Impact_of_Situational_Awareness_Attributes_for_Resilience_Assessment_of_Active_Distribution_Networks_Using_Hybrid_Dynamic_Bayesian_Multi_Criteria_Decision-making_Approach

[177] 'Situational awareness – A lever to face challenges and build resilience', BCI blog, 20 November 2023.
https://www.thebci.org/news/bci-blog-situational-awareness-a-lever-to-face-challenges-and-build-resilience.html

[178] Darwin, J. and Melling, A. (2011) 'Mindfulness and situation awareness', 16th ICCRTS 'C2 for Complex Endeavours' Paper Number 040.
https://www.researchgate.net/profile/John-Darwin-2/publication/235091729_Mindfulness_and_Situation_Awareness/links/5513d0ac0cf2eda0df302d40/Mindfulness-and-Situation-Awareness.pdf

[179] Needham-Bennett, C. and Banks, G. (2023) 'Retrospective: unveiling overlooked challenges to resilience', Resilience First.
https://resiliencefirst.org/news/2023-retrospective-unveiling-overlooked-challenges-to-resilience/

[180] Mackenzie, P. (2021) 'Build back stronger – the final report of renew normal: the people's commission on life

after COVID-19', p. 22, Demos.
https://demos.co.uk/research/build-back-stronger/
[181] Gibbon, E. (2020) *The History of the Decline and Fall of the Roman Empire*, Chapter 3, Penguin Classics. ISBN: 9780140437645.
https://www.ccel.org/g/gibbon/decline/volume1/chap3.htm
[182] Hall, R. Ibid.
[183] 'Social change model of leadership development', UC San Diego, Hawaii.
https://www.heri.ucla.edu/PDFs/pubs/ASocialChangeModel ofLeadershipDevelopment.pdf
[184] Aurelius, M. Ibid, Book 7.

Chapter 9

[185] Kierkegaard, S. (2008) *Journalen* JJ:167, Princeton University Press. ISBN: 9780691133447.
[186] Quote attributed to Tariq Ali Khan, the Pakistani-British intellectual and writer.
[187] De Tocqueville, A. Ibid. Volume 2, Part 4, Chapter 8.
[188] 'There are 50 million more girls in school today than in 2015', GEM Report, UNESCO, 11 October 2023.
https://world-education-blog.org/2023/10/11/there-are-50-million-more-girls-in-school-today-than-in-2015/
[189] Peyton-Jones, T. (2023) 'Speech to the foundation for science and technology'.
https://www.foundation.org.uk/Events/2023/Risk-and-Resilience-Foundation-Future-Leaders-Conf
[190] Ansell, B. Ibid.

[191] Aurelius, M. Ibid, Book 6.

[192] Sagarin, R. (2012) *Learning from the Octopus*, Basic Books. ISBN: 9780465021833.

[193] Popper, K. (2002) *The Open Society and its Enemies*, Routledge Classics. ISBN: 9780415290630

[194] BTI, Ibid.

[195] Proust, M. (2023) *The Captive*, Zinc Read. ISBN: 9789358852042.

[196] Quote attributed to Robert Louis Stevenson, the novelist.

Index

absorb 70, 73, 80, 127
adapt .. 15, 17, 22, 31, 45, 70, 75, 80, 93, 106, 120, 125, 126, 128, 130, 136, 152, 159, 164, 167
adaptability 14, 16, 24, 30, 42, 75, 128, 167
adaptation 27, 30, 37, 43, 46, 68, 70, 86, 121, 122, 125, 126, 127, 128, 129, 159, 161, 162, 166, 168
agile ... 16, 46, 118, 122, 123, 125, 128, 140, 150, 164
agility 14, 27, 30, 68, 97, 121, 122, 123, 124, 125, 126, 129, 134, 140, 164, 166, 167
Agility 194
amygdala 53, 54
Andrews, I 94, 102
anticipate . 16, 21, 22, 58, 61, 70, 71, 114, 127, 137, 170
antifragile 19

antithesis 121
anxiety .. 52, 53, 75, 113, 139
anxiety, age of 21
apatheia (peace of mind) . 88
Aristotle 33, 81, 88, 119, 121, 126, 130, 131, 136, 188, 195
artificial intelligence . 20, 27, 39, 51, 85, 115, 124, 168
Aurelius 180, 199, 200
Aurelius, M ... 33, 39, 40, 42, 48, 152, 154, 161, 162
axiology 25

Bateson, G 125
benediction of enough 28, 79
Brewer 189, 190
Brewer, R 92, 93, 94, 100
building back better strategy 22
Burke, E 74

change 21, 22, 23, 24, 25, 30, 31, 46, 49, 50, 52, 57, 58, 66, 70, 87, 96, 97, 105, 117, 118, 119, 120, 121, 122, 126, 128, 129, 130, 132, 140, 142, 145, 146, 150, 152, 153, 161, 163, 167, 169, 170, 180, 194, 199
change, behavioural 159, 160, 168
change, climate 19, 20, 39, 41, 97, 127, 162
change, demographic 80
chaos theory (butterfly effect) 18
Cicero, M 78
Clark, C 50
coalitions of the willing 83
collectivist attitudes 38
communication 112, 141, 142, 143, 144, 168, 197
community resilience 40, 109
confluence of connectedness 42, 160
Confucius 67
corporate culture 92
corporate memory 74
corporate social responsibility (CSR) ... 93, 102, 153
Corporate Sustainability Reporting Directive (CSRD) 97
courage ... 29, 67, 68, 69, 70, 75, 76, 86, 88, 96, 98, 120, 153
COVID-19, pre-COVID . 18, 19, 20, 61, 84, 96, 101, 110, 129, 143, 144, 145, 150, 151, 152, 157, 162, 165
culture 15, 24, 27, 29, 36, 37, 38, 39, 44, 47, 56, 62, 64, 68, 87, 90, 92, 99, 100, 108, 135, 141, 139
culture, code / statement 100

Darwin 198
Darwin, C 126, 167
De Tocqueville, A 51, 156
defence cascade 53
degrowth theory 79
democratic recession 158
Descartes, R 136, 145
Dewey, J 125, 133, 137
dialectical process 121
Diamond, J 91
diversity 100, 126, 140
Diviney, R 111
doctrine 33, 98
dopamine 54
Dweck, C 133

dwelling in advance..........59
Dyer, W..........................118

efficiency............80, 81, 124
ego strength......................76
Einstein, A.................73, 105
Eisenhower, D..........87, 144
Empedocles.....................126
empowerment..90, 117, 123, 127, 135, 162, 167
environment, sustainability and governance (ESG) + R..............................93, 97
Epictetus.......35, 48, 88, 155
Epicureanism, philosophy of...................................49
Epicurus...........................49
epistemology............25, 136
ethics....67, 88, 94, 145, 191
ethics, descriptive..............68
ethics, normative..............68
ethics, situational............145
ethics, virtue...............67, 68
eudaimonia (living well)..88
existentialism, philosophy of...................................88

facts, alternative......115, 116
fear and superstition.........28
fear of solitude.................49
fear setting..................58, 59
fear, absence of *(ataraxia)*49

fear, culture of............ 56, 62
fear, heuristics of............. 56
fear, philosophy of..... 27, 52
fears, groundless........ 28, 55
Ferriss, T........................... 58
Fink................................. 189
Fink, L........................ 93, 97
flight or fight............ 53, 122
foresight....... 16, 59, 70, 168
Freedman, L..................... 71
Fukushima (nuclear accident).................... 126
Fukuyama, F.................. 106

Galileo........................... 145
general will............ 103, 108
Gibbon, E....................... 152
Gini coefficient................ 83
global............................. 186
governance.... 129, 149, 152, 153, 161, 169
governance, collective..... 82
governance, global.... 20, 66, 82, 128, 161
greenwashing................... 97

hard skills... 14, 31, 134, 135
Hegel, G......... 121, 122, 170
Heidegger, M................. 169
Heraclitus of Ephesus... 119, 120
hindsight 70, 72, 73, 74, 140

hippocampus 54
Hobbes, T 108
holism, holistic 39, 40, 44, 45, 160, 163
Huntington, S 65

imaginal discs 130
imagination, failure / lack of 73, 74, 141
impact, social 92
impacts 28
individualism, individualistic .37, 38, 40, 160
inequality 83, 84, 109, 187
insight 25, 27, 32, 34, 48, 59, 70, 74, 75, 121, 127, 140, 143, 168, 171, 172

James, W 125
Jonas, H 56
Jung, C 120
just in case 124
just in time 15, 124
just war 77
justice 29, 68, 69, 70, 78, 81, 82, 83, 84, 108

Kant, I 18, 52, 137, 140
Khan Review 109, 166
Kierkegaard 199

Kierkegaard, S .. 11, 26, 140, 142, 155, 171
King Charles III 96
Kipling, R 77
knowledge (epistemology) 16, 24, 25, 28, 31, 34, 57, 67, 70, 88, 105, 116, 130, 131, 136, 137, 138, 139, 140, 141, 157, 165, 167, 168
kosmopolites (cosmoplitans) 39
Kruger, D 110

Lao-Tzu 68
Lauritzen, P 130, 131
leadership 21, 27, 42, 43, 47, 66, 71, 90, 99, 100, 101, 102, 104, 107, 110, 112, 113, 128, 129, 134, 146, 149, 152, 153, 161, 163, 165, 169
learning . 47, 72, 73, 74, 120, 127, 131, 133, 134, 135, 136, 137, 138, 139, 140, 141, 168
learning by doing 137
legislation 85
list of values (LOV) 95
Locke, J 107, 108, 136, 137, 142, 145
logic 25, 75, 134

Lorenz concept 18
Lorenz, E 18

Machiavelli, N 132
Marx(ism) 121, 170
Massumi, B 52
McAslan, A 80
McLeod, C 107
Mehrabian, A 143
Melville, H 28
metamorphosis 129
metaphysics 25, 115
meta-skills 31, 136, 167, 168
mindfulness . 14, 36, 69, 148, 157, 159, 180
mindset, concept of ... 24, 25, 122, 133, 135, 146, 148, 152
moderation 29, 68, 69, 70, 76, 77, 80
moral compass ... 29, 91, 104, 143, 156
moral excellence. 67, 88, 102
mutually intertwined movements 40, 42, 161

narcissism 44
National Risk Register 60
nationalism 43
Needham-Bennett ... 184, 198
Needham-Bennett, C 63, 150
Nietzsche, F 88, 89

normative 68
north star 71, 152

Ockham's Razor 116, 163
O'Donohue, J 36
oikeiosis (familiarisation) 41
Oliver 180, 181
Oliver, T 37, 38, 39, 42
open society 169

Parmar 183, 185
Parmar, R 69, 72
Peckham, R 50
perception, philosophy of 144, 145
performance .. 47, 80, 92, 97, 132, 150
Performance 181
permacrisis 32
philosophy, concept of 25, 26
phobias 49
phobos (phobias) 49
Plato 33, 68, 69, 88, 121, 136, 170, 185
plausibility 62
polarisation . 29, 31, 78, 109, 113, 114, 165
polis (city-state) 39
poly-crisis 32, 128
Popper 200
Popper, K 121, 137, 169, 170

populism, populist.....21, 43, 65, 162
possibility...........62, 63, 184
post-traumatic stress disorder (PTSD)............53
precautionary principle / culture.....................57, 62
prefrontal cortex................54
preparation 71, 110, 138, 163, 168
probability 59, 60, 61, 62, 63, 184
proof of vigour 120
proportionality.............77, 78
Proust, M.........................170
Publicly Available Specification (PAS) 92
purpose (see also vision).33, 34, 36, 70, 76, 88, 91, 92, 93, 94, 99, 100, 102, 110, 123, 125, 127, 141, 146, 149, 150

quantum technologies / computing 27, 51, 168

real risk..............................63
reasonable worst-case scenario (RWCS)...60, 61
recession of the spirit 21, 158
reductionism, reductionist 37, 39

redundancy 15, 81, 124, 164, 167
regulation....................... 185
regulation(s)... 52, 64, 85, 91
reliability........80, 81, 90, 112
resilience mindset(s). 29, 31, 47, 48, 58, 87, 152, 155, 158, 167, 171
resilience of the extremes 43, 78
resilience strategy 71, 72, 164
resilience, Chinese concept of 24
resilience, concept / philosophy of.. 20, 21, 22, 29, 66, 75, 164
resilience, Russian concept of 23
resistance 22, 23, 24, 30, 35, 39, 120, 153, 166
resistance, anti-microbial. 39
risk appetite . 59, 63, 64, 183
risk matrix........................ 60
risk tolerance 63
risk-industrial complex .. 163
risks, causes, consequences / impacts 27, 28, 32, 45, 59, 162
river of flux.................... 119
Roberts........... 185, 186, 195
Roberts, A............. 66, 80, 81

robustness 22, 23, 140
Rogers, B 144
Roosevelt, F D 54
Rousseau, J-J 103, 108
Rubin, T 70

Saint Aquinas, T 77, 122, 136
Saint Augustine 77
Samuel, J 120
SARS-CoV-2 18
Sartre, J-P 88
scenario (RWCS) 61
Schwartz Value Survey 95
Schwartz, S 95
Seldon, A 138
self-awareness . 17, 145, 146, 148, 149, 197
Seligman, M 40
Seneca, L .. 55, 56, 68, 77, 81
Shea, J 45
Sherman, N 38, 40, 42, 43, 46
single-issue networks 83
situational awareness 28, 117, 145, 146, 147, 148, 198
skillset 133
social capital ... 106, 151, 191
Social Change Model of Leadership 153
social contract 108

social covenant 110
social impact 92
social skills 149, 150, 151
Socrates 33, 88, 136, 140, 141
Socratic Paradox 140
soft skills. 31, 134, 135, 150, 168
Spiegelhalter, D 143
Spinoza, B 48, 49
stakeholder capitalism 93, 102
stewardship. 85, 94, 97, 101, 102, 164
Stoicism, philosophy 26, 27, 33, 120
Stoicism, Stoics, Stoic 25, 28, 29, 33, 34, 35, 36, 38, 39, 41, 42, 44, 45, 46, 47, 51, 58, 59, 67, 68, 74, 79, 81, 88, 89, 108, 120, 141, 145, 148, 154, 157, 159, 170
strategy 99, 111, 144, 147
sustainability. 77, 79, 80, 93, 97, 102, 132
Svendsen, L 52, 105
Syed, M 89
synthesis 121, 122

Taleb, N 14, 19, 75
Taoism 68

Thales of Miletus 118
The Prince's Trust 51
theory of forms 126
theory of knowledge 136
thesis 121
Thomism, philosophy of .. 77
transformation(al),
transformative .22, 26, 36, 70, 127, 129, 130, 160, 161
transient caretakers 94
translational leaders 47
Truss, L 83
trust 7, 15, 29, 30, 46, 51, 101, 105, 106, 107, 109, 111, 112, 113, 114, 116, 117, 134, 135, 141, 149, 150, 165, 166, 180, 191, 192
trustworthiness .. 46, 90, 107, 139, 192
truth ... 15, 25, 29, 38, 69, 72, 74, 90, 105, 106, 107, 113, 114, 115, 116, 117, 120, 137, 142, 165, 166, 193
truth, battle for 113
truth, post- 114, 116

UK Resilience
Framework 111

UK Stewardship Code
(2020) 101
universal soul 162
ustoichivost (robustness).. 23

value(s) (axiology).... 14, 16, 24, 25, 28, 29, 36, 37, 62, 68, 70, 87, 88, 89, 91, 92, 93, 97, 99, 101, 102, 103, 104, 107, 113, 129, 146, 151, 153, 156, 157, 158, 162, 169
values, ethical 90, 94, 96, 100, 102, 163
values, set of . 29, 76, 94, 96, 98
Vierci, P 26
virtue(s) .. 29, 35, 40, 46, 47, 67, 68, 69, 70, 81, 86, 87, 88, 104, 136, 145, 152, 156, 157, 158, 162
Virtue-based Psycho-social Adaptation Model (V-PAM) 86
virtus (virtue) 34
vision 14, 17, 71, 72, 91, 93, 96, 100, 102, 111, 113, 145, 152, 158, 161, 163
von Bertalanffy, L 125
VUCA 167

war on terrorism 78

whole of nation. 40, 111, 151
whole of society ..40, 84, 85, 92, 111, 151, 160
Wildavsky, A 27, 28
will to power 89
William of Ockham........116
Wilson, E..........................32

wisdom 7, 25, 29, 68, 69, 70, 73, 75, 86, 88, 120, 130, 152, 157, 159, 183
Wolff's Law...................... 19

Zeno of Citium 33
zero risk 62, 64
Zuckerberg, M 96